LEARN
FROM THE
MASTER

By Wayne Augustine M.Ed.
with a special chapter by Pastor James P. Augustine

INTRODUCTION

The book of Matthew is looked upon by many theologians as the Gospel written from a Jewish perspective, primarily to present Jesus to the Jewish nation as their promised Messiah. A number of the teachings of Jesus reported by Matthew are difficult to understand until a look at Jewish customs and practices are taken into consideration.

But while Matthew's purpose in writing this gospel was to present their King, the Lord Jesus, to the Jewish People, the Holy Spirit may have had an additional purpose in mind: that of demonstrating to all believers what it will take to become a real and effective disciple of the Lord Jesus along with the training necessary to accomplish this. As you read this manuscript, my hope is that you will grasp this concept and actually put it into practice. Those of you who do will be the key to reaching the world for Christ in one generation and only a few are needed to make it happen.

The purpose of this writing is to open up the Book of Matthew in a very practical way. The text of this book is meant to clarify the scriptures in much the same way that a pastor preaches and clarifies the Word of God on a Sunday morning. Therefore it is essential that throughout your study, you constantly read through the Book of Matthew so that the Holy Spirit can help you in your understanding of real discipleship. I believe that most of you will see the application and the intent of Jesus as He prepares His disciples for ministry and it is for you that I will be praying: praying that God will bless your efforts as we obey Christ's great commission to 'Go to all the world and preach the Gospel (to every creature), teaching them to observe all that Christ commanded' and remember His promise to us: "I am with you always, even to the ends of the earth!" (Matthew 28:20)

TABLE OF CONTENTS

DEDICATION

I would like to dedicate this book to my wife Mary and my two sons, Timothy and James whom God used to enhance our ministry throughout the last forty-seven years. When preaching to my congregation, or in another church, or in a camp setting, or in presenting our Family Foundations Seminars throughout the area, their presence always made the message so much stronger, because of their willingness to let the Holy Spirit work through them as they ministered along with me. And now, even as Mary and I continue to work together, Tim and Jim have families of their own, with whom they work to do the will of the Master.

I will always be thankful to God for the blessing of my wife and our two sons, and for the wives and children of our sons. To all of them, I dedicate this book.

CHAPTER ONE

MULTITUDES FOLLOWED HIM, SO WHY DOES HE NEED DISCIPLES?

By the time you have finished reading this book you will know that <u>you</u> have the potential to impact the more than six billion people on the earth for Christ. You will know that it is possible to accomplish this in the next thirty-three to thirty five years even if you live only a few more years. You will have a greater understanding of the characteristics that constitute a real disciple and you will realize that by laying aside a few extra hours each week, investing your life in only a few people, you could actually change the world for Christ in a generation.

In order to accomplish this it will be necessary to understand what a disciple is by definition. What did Jesus mean when He issued the 'GREAT COMMISSION?' In Matthew 28:19, Jesus, addressing His disciples tells them to go and make disciples of all nations. From His words, the definition is very clear. He is addressing His disciples and He instructs them to make disciples. Therefore, a true disciple is a believer in Jesus Christ who views that his/her primary purpose in life is to make disciples!

You will probably need to read the book several times to clearly catch the vision, so let's get started!

The Book of Matthew was clearly written by Matthew to present the Gospel of Christ to the Nation of Israel. A phrase often found in the Book is, "…that it might fulfill that which was spoken by the prophets…" or some similar phrase intended to help the Jewish people to see many of the Old Testament prophecies fulfilled in the life of Jesus. We dare not diminish the truth of this perspective for Jesus came first to the Jewish nation. In John, chapter one, verse twelve, John writes, "He came unto His own and His own received Him not." Paul writes in Romans, chapter one and verse 16, "…to the Jew first, and also to the Greek (Gentile)." While Matthew is concerned for the Jewish nation, the Holy Spirit is focusing on the whole world as He prepares the twelve for discipleship. Matthew's presentation of Jesus' teaching is for the Gentiles as well. The men Jesus chose to teach and to become His disciples in the beginning were all Jews so it is fitting that in the writings of Matthew we see Christ's plan for training His disciples and all disciples.

Matthew begins his book by establishing the assigned earthly father's lineage all the way back to Abraham: God's promise fulfilled. Even though Joseph was the adoptive father, assigned by God to care for Mary and the Baby Jesus, his lineage is vital to Biblical prophesy. Joseph plays a key role in the life of Christ and therefore his lineage is every bit as important as that of Mary and perhaps even more so in the Jewish culture. Matthew records some information of Christ's birth and some miracles surrounding that event including God's intervention in saving Him from the wrath of Herod. God's voice affirms Jesus' identity in chapter three as Christ is baptized by John the Baptist in the wilderness. Chapter four records His wilderness experience where He is tempted by satan, but is victorious on all counts.

Toward the middle of chapter four, Jesus calls His disciples to follow Him and then toward the end of the chapter we are told that the multitudes followed Him everywhere He traveled. He has the attention of thousands of people, so WHY DOES HE NEED DISCIPLES?

We must never lose sight of Christ's love for the multitudes. "For God so loved the <u>world</u> that He gave His only begotten Son, that whosoever believeth in Him should not perish, but have everlasting life. For God sent not His Son into the <u>world</u> to condemn the <u>world</u>, but that the <u>world</u> through Him might be saved." (John 3:16-17) "…but (God) is longsuffering toward us, not willing that any should perish, but that <u>all</u> should come to repentance" (II Peter 3:9). We note the broken heart of Jesus as He laments over Jerusalem, "O Jerusalem, Jerusalem, which kills the prophets and stones them that are sent unto you, how often would I have gathered your children together, as a hen gathers her brood under her wings, and you would not." (Luke 13:34)

In chapter five of Matthew's gospel we see Jesus, again seeing the multitudes of people. If we meditate upon the words, "and seeing the multitudes" for a period of time, we can sense His great love for each of them (that whosoever of John 3:16). Yet in this instance He does not focus on the multitudes at all. Instead He calls His disciples to Him and begins to teach them, not the multitudes. Why? Because

Jesus knew that under God's plan, He could not reach the multitudes in three years or in a hundred years by Himself. He would build His Church (Matthew 16:18), but He would build it via His disciples and so He begins to train them here in chapter five. Jesus knew that His Church could never become a reality through addition. It could only grow and prosper through multiplication. People who came to Him during His earthly ministry were only added to His followers; to multiply required discipleship.

So in His final instruction to His disciples, Jesus does not ask them to win souls, although that is included. Instead He calls on them to make disciples ("all power is given unto Me in heaven and in earth. Go ye therefore, and teach all nations, baptizing them in the name of the Father, and of the Son, and of the Holy Spirit: teaching them to observe all things whatsoever I have commanded you..."). An individual who has not acknowledged Jesus as the only hope for his sin problem cannot be His disciple. But once having placed his hope in the Savior, he can only be a disciple if he is trained to be a disciple. So as Jesus trained His twelve disciples, let Him now train you. And we are going to learn the important characteristics of a disciple from Matthews's gospel and from the teachings of Christ Himself.

Jesus begins His teaching by talking about attitudes. He lists them at the beginning of chapter five and I believe that a key verse in all His training is found in 5:20, "For I say unto you, except your righteousness shall exceed the righteousness of the scribes and Pharisees, you shall in no case enter into the kingdom of heaven." Our attitude impacts everything we do. Attitudes effect how we do what we are doing. Attitude effects how others perceive and receive what we do or communicate. Our attitude is caught by others around us and can positively or negatively impact the attitudes of others which will influence their response to the Gospel message.

Several years ago, while watching a playoff game between the Florida Marlins and the Chicago Cubs, Mary and I were enjoying the fact that the Cubs had a commanding lead in the series and in the game that we were watching. Then the famous foul fly was hit into the left field stands and as the Cubs outfielder was reaching into the stands for the catch, a fan reached for the ball, knocking the ball away from the player and the out was not made. As that outfielder returned to his position, his attitude was total dejection: he was convinced that the missed opportunity would cost the Cubs the game. His obvious dejection spread to the rest of the team, to the people in the stadium, to those watching on television and ultimately to the entire city of Chicago. The fan's life was threatened, the game was lost and the Marlins won the playoff, eliminating the Cubs from contention, and went on to win the World Series. All this happened in part due to the attitude of one player who, by the way, probably believed in the myth of the Chicago Cub's curse.

This author, as he watched the dejected outfielder return to his position, turned to his wife, Mary, an ardent Cubs fan still to this very day, and said, "The series is over, the Cubs have lost," and they did! Their only hope was for their manager to lead them in a change of attitude which did not happen. I'm certain he tried, but the attitude was too entrenched in the minds of the players and there was not enough time to accomplish the task. I'm sure that to this day many still blame that fan for the loss: for doing what most fans would have done, gone for a souvenir of a Cub's playoff game in Chicago. Real champions can only be champions if they have the right attitude.

What would have happened to the Cubs in that series had the outfielder turned to the fan and said, "Nice catch!" and returned to his position thinking, "That fan made an incredible effort! Thank God for our fans!" Then continued to play with the attitude of confidence he had played with all year. They probably would have been world champions. And if one missed foul ball could derail their chances for a world title, then they were not real champions anyway.

Continuing to use sports as an illustration, a number of years ago a famous coach began to change the face of athletic competition with the statement, "Winning is not everything, it is the only thing." Coaches, players, owners of franchises and fans have adopted this phrase and as a result the game has radically changed. You see, if winning is, "the only thing" then nothing else matters. You must do whatever it takes to win; teach players to break the rules of the game to gain an unfair advantage, take drugs to give your self the edge even though it is illegal, pay officials to lean your way in the heat of competition, or anything else that can give you an advantage you did not earn. When caught, these players may not be named to the "Hall of Fame" but the sin is in getting caught, not in attempting to gain the undeserved advantage.

As a coach, this author never asked his players to win. Was winning a goal? Of course it was, but it was not the most important goal. Players were never asked to win. They were asked to give their best at all times. A quote they heard often was, "He is no great athlete who gives his best when he feels like it; anybody can do that. Rather he is a real athlete who gives his best when he doesn't feel like it. Does your body control you, or are you in control of your body? Do you serve your body or does your body serve you?"

When you give your best at all times your chance of winning is two out of three. If you are the best team and you give your best, you will win. If you give your best and you are not the best team and your opponent gives his best, you will lose. If you give your best and your opponent is better than you are, but does not give his best, you will win. Find ways to praise your opponent when he beats you and find ways to praise him when you beat him. It will help you in future competition. It is all about attitude!

Many teams have lost games because they believed that, "Winning is the only thing." When a team enjoys a large lead, their attitude includes the thought, "We've won," so they let up, no longer interested in giving their best. Their opponent is not convinced that the game is over and by the time the leaders are aware that their lead is diminishing, they find themselves behind in the score and often cannot regain the momentum. As long as this attitude prevails in the world of sports, we can not use the game to teach character and values. Instead we are teaching that the end justifies the means and that is never right! What far reaching impacts an attitude can have on everything we attempt? We're talking about attitudes!

Jesus understood the importance of one's attitude, so He begins to train at the beginning. He talks about attitudes. We call them, "The Beatitudes." Do everything absolutely correct, but with the wrong attitude, and your effectiveness will be greatly diminished. In the next several chapters we are going to look at each of these attitudes as Jesus presents them. We will define them and ask ourselves, "How do my attitudes measure up?" Your attitude can make or break you as you purpose to live in obedience to Christ.

CHAPTER TWO

WRONG ATTITUDES CAN
WEAKEN OUR EFFECTIVENESS

Jesus, seeing the multitudes and knowing that one day His disciples will need to, "…Go into all the world and preach the Gospel to every creature," (Mark 16:15) begins to prepare the twelve for their very vital task: to be instruments of the Master in building His church. A very important aspect of their preparation is that they approach the multitudes with the right attitude. To do things right with the wrong attitude can actually grieve the Holy Spirit and interfere with that which He wants to accomplish in a person's life. The goal of Jesus is to reach the multitudes, but to accomplish this He must train the disciples. There are nine "Blesseds" so we are going to look at nine attitudes. You may find more as you read through Matthew. Some interface with each other. The number is not important. The attitude is important! Jesus begins His teaching:

I. "Blessed are the poor in spirit: for theirs is the Kingdom of Heaven" (Matthew 5:3)

While these attitudes may not be listed in the order of their importance, this author sees them as equally vital to the task at hand. No one attitude is more important than another. A chain is no stronger than its weakest link. As we allow the Holy Spirit to strengthen each of them in our lives, we will proportionally become more effective in accomplishing God's great plan to reach the world for Christ.

Jesus begins with humility, Poor in spirit. In Luke 14 Jesus is speaking of a wedding when He admonishes the disciples to take the lower seat, "For whosoever exalts himself shall be abased, but whosoever humbles himself shall be exalted." Again in Luke 18:14 when speaking of the exhibitions of worship displayed by the Pharisee and the publican, he says again, "...for everyone that exalts himself shall be abased, and he that humbles himself shall be exalted." Peter, in his first Epistle writes in chapter five, verses five through seven, "...for God resists the proud, and gives grace to the humble. Humble yourselves therefore under the mighty hand of God, that He may exalt you in due time, casting all your care upon Him, for He cares for you."

The writer of Proverbs reminds us in Chapter 6, verses 16 and 17 that God hates pride. "These six things doth the Lord hate: yea seven are an abomination to the Lord," and the first on the list is 'a proud look.' Pride often interferes with the very thing God is leading us to do. God prompts us to ask forgiveness of someone who has wronged us, but our pride says, "He should come to me!" Jesus tells His disciples in Matthew 5, verses 23 and 24; if you are about to worship, and suddenly remember that there is someone who has something against you (not you against them, them against you!), leave your gift, go, make things right, then you can come back and worship. When sharing Christ with others, a feeling of pride, the feeling that I am better than those without Christ, will come through loud and clear, thus blocking the message from the one who may need it desperately.

Let me attempt to define humility. One definition is this: 'All that I am and all that I will ever accomplish is the result of what God and God through others have accomplished in my life.' When we look at our lives and realize that we are but sinners saved by God's grace, we realize that there is no room for pride in our lives whatsoever. One day a young boy asked his Father, "Dad, how far is the sun away from the earth?" The Father replied, "About ninety-three million miles." After mulling the answer over in his mind for a brief time, he asked, "Is that measured from the upstairs window or the downstairs window?" When we begin to think that our walk with the Lord transcends the walk of many others, just remember that the difference between the most righteous human being who ever lived and the greatest sinner who ever walked the face of the earth, in the sight of God is the difference of ninety-three million miles measured from the upstairs window compared to the measurement from the downstairs window. For God has decreed that all have sinned and come short of the glory of God.

Because of our sinful nature, pride will be a constant battle. It will prevent us from speaking to someone about Christ when urged to do so by the Spirit of God: or from meeting a need in someone's life because we are too busy with other 'necessary' things: or from living in obedience to the Holy Spirit when what is on our own agenda seems so much more important.

I remember a story my father used to tell as I listened to him preach when I was young. A famous preacher was traveling on a train headed for a very important assignment to speak in a very large church. As the train sped on its way he realized that he was not as prepared as he needed to be and so was going over his notes as he rode toward his destination. At one stop he noticed a man with seven small children get on the train and sit down across the aisle from him, attempting to keep order with the kids. The pastor thought it strange that he would travel with all those children without the mother. The Holy Spirit prompted him to go and talk with the man, but his message was important. It would bolster his career if delivered correctly, so he ignored the Holy Spirit and continued to study for his most important assignment. Several hours passed and finally he felt good about his preparation, so he put the notes and his Bible aside and got up and approached the man with the seven children. He picked up the child seated next to the man he assumed to be the father and sat down. "I could not help but notice as you got on the train that you were traveling with all these children and did not bring their mother," he spoke trying to open up a conversation that would enable him to minister to the family. The man looked at him appreciatively and said, "O, she is with us. She is in the baggage coach. We are taking her back to the little town where we met and where I married her to lay her to rest." With that the train began to slow down and the man said, "This is where we get off." The Pastor helped him corral the children, assisted him with the bags they had carried on with them, helped them off the train and waved good-bye. He watched as the coffin was rolled across the station platform, followed by the man and his children. As he went back to his seat and the train began to move again, his message no longer seemed so important His pride, his message, what he thought was so vital to his future, now paled in comparison against the opportunity he had missed which may have been the very reason God had placed him on the train. His heart was broken. He prayed for forgiveness.

JESUS SAID THAT TO BE ALL GOD WANTS YOU TO BE, TO BE THE MOST EFFECTIVE DISCIPLE, YOU MUST BE HUMBLE!

2. "Blessed are they that mourn: for they shall be comforted." (Matthew 5:4)

Here Jesus is speaking about our attitude toward sin. God hates sin: we must hate it, too. When we see sin, we should weep. Sin should break our hearts because it results in death. Romans 3:23 reminds us that, "The wages of sin is death…" Ezekiel tells us in chapter 18, verse 20, "The soul that sins, it shall die!"

The problem is that we are born with a sinful nature, and as a result, tend to be drawn to it. In Romans seven, Paul outlines our struggle: 'what I want to do, what I know is the right thing to do, I don't do and what I hate and know to be wrong, I find myself doing.' As with pride, this too will be a constant battle. Of course the answer Paul concludes is in verses 24 and 25. He describes his dilemma with these words: "O wretched man that I am! Who shall deliver me from the body of this death?" In Paul's day a common punishment for murder was carried out by tying the body of the deceased to the one who had taken his life, hands tied to hands, feet tied to feet, bound face to face to that decomposing body being compelled to carry it where ever he went. This is the illustration Paul is using to describe our sin nature and the people of Rome understood what he meant. What an awful thought, yet an accurate picture of sin. He asks, "How do I escape?" "I thank God through Jesus Christ our Lord! So then with the mind I myself serve the law of God, but with the flesh the law of sin." To attempt to defeat sin in our lives using our own strength and ability is a formula for certain defeat. But to allow the power of the Holy Spirit to empower us, and to constantly remind us that we are no match by ourselves to overcome the sin that is within us, will allow us to experience victory over sin and to say, with Paul, "I thank God through Jesus Christ our Lord!"

Let's go back to Romans chapter six to see how this works out in practice. Paul points out that when we became believers in Christ, we became dead to sin. In verses 3 through 7 he writes, "Know you not that so many of us as were baptized into Jesus Christ were baptized into His death? Therefore we are buried with Him by baptism unto death: that like as Christ was raised up from the dead by the glory of the Father, even so we also should walk in newness of life. For if we have been planted together in the likeness of His death, we shall be also in the likeness of His resurrection. Knowing this, that our old man is crucified with Him, that the body of sin might be destroyed, that henceforth we should not serve sin. For he that is dead is freed from sin!" The illustration is that dead people do not sin nor are they even tempted to sin. Take a delicious dinner into a funeral home and place it near the deceased and what will he do? Nothing! He's dead! He cannot respond. Bring in a scantily clad woman past the dead male and how will he respond? He won't. Why? Because he is dead, he can't respond. That is the way death tends to affect us. Paul is telling us that once we are 'in Christ' we are essentially dead to sin.

But there is a problem. At true conversion we are redeemed by the blood of Christ, however, as great a miracle as that is, our bodies are not redeemed. In Romans 8 we are told in verse 15 that we have received the 'Spirit of Adoption' and then in verse 23 we are informed that along with the world, we groan in our flesh, waiting for the adoption which is the redemption of the body. Clearly, when salvation comes to us, we are redeemed, but our bodies are not. Therefore we will experience the struggle Paul refers to in chapter seven of Romans. How do we deal with this struggle in a practical way? Paul tells us in the remainder of chapter six.

We are to visualize ourselves as dead to sin, believe that we are dead to sin, and then act like we are dead to sin. An act of our will, empowered by the Holy Spirit, determined to hate even the thought of sin, will go far in helping us to overcome temptation. There are many sins that do not even come close to tempting us. These are the ones we tend to see in others and then judge them for their lack of ability to overcome them. There are others to which we are so vulnerable that we often excuse them telling ourselves that everyone struggles with these temptations.

How are we to deal with temptation according to chapter six? Paul gives us a simple formula for victory. In verses twelve and following we are told to refuse to allow sin to rule our unredeemed bodies. We are not to use the members of our body as instruments to sin, but rather we are to yield our body to God and its members as instruments of righteousness, knowing that we have been raised from the dead with Christ. You are a Child of God. Sin is not to have the rule over your life. Why? Because you are dead to sin! He goes on to warn us in verses 16 and following; what you do with the members of your body will determine to what you will become enslaved. We all serve something. The question is who or what will we serve? If you use the members of your body to sin, you will become the servant of sin. If, on the other hand, you chose to use the members of your body as instruments to accomplish the good and righteous acts that will bring honor to the Lord Jesus Christ, you will then become the servant of righteousness. If you decide to choose to serve sin, you will be free from righteousness. (This also would be a good reason to examine your self, whether you are really in the faith II Corinthians 13:5). You then need to ask yourself, "What positive results can I show from the years I gave sin the priority in my life (verse 21)? But if you choose to serve God and the things pleasing to Him, you will bear fruit unto holiness and bring others to everlasting life.

How can you tell if you truly hate sin? One way is to take a critical look at how you view sinners. Do they disgust you? Are they appalling to you? Do you want to be as far away from them as possible? Then it is not sin that you hate, but sinners. When we hate sinners it is most likely because they remind us of our own sinfulness and so we vent against them in order to take the focus off ourselves.

Jesus hates sin, but loves sinners. He spent much of His time with them. In fact, one of the problems the religious leaders had with Christ was the fact that He hung out with sinners and even ate with them.

A little girl ran home from Sunday school and ran to her mother and said, "Mother, my name is in the Bible!" Her Mother put her arms around her and told her that the names of Mary, Martha, Joanna, Sarah are there but the name 'Edith' is not a Biblical name. "O, yes it is, Mother. My teacher told us this morning that this man Jesus receives sinners and eateth with them" (Luke 15:2 KJV)!

I like that story because I can put my name in there. This man, Jesus receives sinners and Wayne with them. This man Jesus receives sinners and _____ (put your name there) with them. To hate sin is to love sinners. It is to hate what sin is doing to those we love. You can hate sin and love sinners, or you can hate sinners because you love sin. You cannot have it both ways.

JESUS SAID THAT TO BE ALL THAT GOD WANTS YOU TO BE, TO BE THE MOST EFFECTIVE DISCIPLE, YOU MUST LEARN TO HATE SIN AND TO FEAR THE DAMAGE THAT IT BRINGS WITH IT.

3. "Blessed are the meek: for they shall inherit the earth." (Matthew 5:5)

It is a shame that the word meek rhymes with weak. People often relate the two which is a gross error. Sometimes a frail little man is referred to as meek, just because he is timid or weak, but this is a vast distortion of the word here in Matthew. A meek person is one who has given to God everything that exists in himself. He has relinquished all of his personal rights and expectations to God and therefore seldom gets angry. His anger is vented only against the sin that he hates, never the sinner. To fully understand the real meaning of the word 'meek,' we must take a close look at human nature.

All of us have a mind set, due to our sinful nature that we are owed certain rights and expectations. When these rights and expectations are withheld, we tend to get upset. Think for a moment about the things that make you angry and you will find, in most cases, that the anger was induced by your failure to receive something you expected or because one of your personal rights was violated. The higher your level of rights and expectations, the more difficult it becomes to make you happy. When the people around you attempt to meet all your expectations, you tend to add more of them to your list, thus eventually reaching a point where it is impossible for people to give you any more, or they just get tired of trying to please you. An illustration of this is the parent who gives his child everything he wants and the result is a spoiled child: a child who is difficult to control. These phenomena, while clearly seen in the parent-child relationship, can also develop between spouses, between employer and employee, between siblings and others.

The meek individual does not get angry or upset. Why? It is because he has given all of his personal rights and expectations to God. He still has rights; he still has expectations, but now he is not looking for the people around him to provide them. Instead he is looking to God to bring them about. Now when things do not happen the way he thinks they should, he knows that, "All things work together for good to them who love God, to them who are called according to His purpose." (Romans 8:28)

His anger is abated for he is trusting in the living God to meet his needs. He is aware that, "God is love" and that "… all good things come from above." If God does not provide something he desires, he knows that God has a good reason. Even though he may have no idea what it is, his trust is in his Master.

When the disciples argued about who would be greatest in the Kingdom of Heaven, Jesus told them that to be great, one must have the heart and mind of a servant (Matthew 23:11). Servants have no rights. Servants have no expectations.

In Luke 17:5-10, in response to the disciple's request to, "Increase our faith," Jesus talks about the thrill of being a servant. When you work all day in the field, and you come home tired and weary, do you sit down and eat? No! You make certain that the master is fed and then you clean up. Do you expect a 'thank you?' No! Because you have only done what a servant should do; you have no expectations from your employer, only from God. The more you know God, the more easily you will trust Him. He desires the best for you.

A number of years ago, I was attending one of Bill Gothard's Pastor's Seminars at Indiana University, (I remember it well because it was the last conference I attended with my father before he died). During one of the sessions, Bill asked a missionary to give a personal testimony about how this principle of meekness had helped him accomplish his goal on the field. The story is in print and I'm certain available through the 'Institute in Basic Youth Conflicts' in Oakbrook, Illinois. The mission assignment was in a tropical country and this missionary had a yearning for pineapples, so he thought that he would plant some for himself and his family. He paid one of the locals to do the planting and three years later, as the pineapples ripened, they began to disappear. After an investigation the missionary discovered that the individual he had hired to do the planting, was now stealing them. When he confronted the culprit, he was told that there was a law in the jungle that basically stated, "He who plants, eats."

"But I paid you to plant them for me" the missionary argued, but to no avail. The answer still came back, "He who plants, eats!"

Finally he told his former employee, "Look, I am going to give you these plants and I will plant new ones." The man asked if he would be paid for digging them up and replanting them at his place.

"Absolutely not" the missionary replied, not just a little bit disturbed. "Then I cannot help you," was the reply.

With great exasperation the missionary set out to dig up all of his pineapple bushes and laid them out by his plot of land. He then purchased new plants and asked another of the locals to plant the pineapples and he agreed.

"Then who will own the bushes after they are planted," he asked?

"You will" he was assured.

"And who will eat the pineapples?' was his next question.

You guessed it! The answer came back, "I will eat the pineapples. It's the law of the jungle, 'he who plants, eats.'

"Never mind," came the reply from a thoroughly frustrated man, called of God to reach a people for Christ. "I'll plant them myself," which he did.

As these new plants became ready for harvesting, once again they began to disappear. It has now been more than seven years since this saga began as pineapples require about three years from planting to harvesting. The locals seemed to like pineapples, too!

So to protect his pineapples, the missionary brought in a large dog which was somewhat effective in the protection process. But eventually his dog cohabited with other dogs in town and the result was more than any of them wanted to deal with, so the guard dog had to go.

Of course the pineapples continued to disappear. As one last ditch effort to protect that which was rightfully his, the missionary closed the clinic and there were no more clothes, food, medicine and other help for the natives so most left the area and moved back to the jungle.

Now the missionary and his family were enjoying their pineapples, but had no ministry. "This makes no sense," he thought. "I can eat pineapples back in the States." So he reopened the clinic, the people came back and the pineapples continued to disappear. Then it was time for the missionary and his family to come home for a furlough.

During his time back home, the star of our story attended a "Basic Youth Conflicts Seminar" led by Bill Gothard and learned the principle of giving everything, all your rights and expectations, to God. As he pondered this concept, he thought, "Maybe I need to give my right to own pineapples to God." Someone had suggested that God could protect the pineapples better than he could protect them!

So upon returning to the mission field, he went out one evening and dedicated his pineapple field and the pineapples to God. His prayer went something like this: "God, all that I own is yours. I guess I had forgotten that that includes these pineapples. So I give You my right to own these pineapples and furthermore, I give each of these pineapples to You. Now Lord, if you can see your way clear to allow me and my family to enjoy a few of these pieces of fruit, that would be nice. But if not, that's okay. They do not belong to me anymore; they are Yours!" Can you guess what happened? That's right! The pineapples continued to disappear! One day he thought, "God, You are not protecting the pineapples any better than I did!"

Several weeks later some of the villagers came to him and said, "Say, you've become a Christian, haven't you?"

The startled missionary tried to explain that he had been a believer in Christ for many years, but they were not convinced. "Why," he asked, "do you think that I have just become a Christian?"

The shocking reply came back, "Because you no longer get angry with us when we steal your pineapples."

The missionary told them that they were no longer his pineapples. He had given them away.

"To whom!" was the startled reply?

"I gave them to God!"

"You did what? You gave them to whom? Why did you do that?"

The locals went back to the village and shared with the others, "Do you know whose pineapples we have been stealing? We have been stealing God's pineapples!" And they stopped stealing the pineapples.

There is an incredible ending to this story. The missionary went to the villagers and told them that he would like to share God's pineapples with them. They could have all of these in this part of the garden, and he and his family would enjoy a few over here, so in the end, the missionary finally got to eat pineapples, and the locals received some as well. But the best news of all is that many of the people the missionary and his family had come to reach for Christ turned to the Lord when they saw the reality of a life completely surrendered to God!

JESUS SAID THAT TO BE AN EFFECTIVE DISCIPLE, TO BE ALL THAT YOU CAN BE, YOU MUST INCLUDE 'MEEKNESS' AS ONE OF THE PRIME PREREQUISITES.

We will continue to study these most important attitudes in chapter three.

CHAPTER THREE

BLESSED MEANS EUPHORIC

The word, 'blessed' in each of these nine attitudes Jesus speaks about is somewhat difficult to understand. When an individual sets out to do a specific task, success brings about a sense of accomplishment and a type of euphoria that often accompanies the successful completion of a task. One of the clearest illustrations in our culture is the athlete who prepares for weeks, plays a sixteen, or eighty-five, or one hundred-sixty game season, struggles through two or three playoff series and finally wins the big one; the Super Bowl, the Stanley Cup, or the World Series. The sense of accomplishment is euphoric, the celebration is incredible, and even though all they have done is 'won a game', the fans, the owners and the players go 'nuts' celebrating the event.

That is close to the meaning of the word, 'blessed' used in these nine attitudes of Jesus. Jesus is getting His disciples ready for the most important task that the world will ever know: the task of bringing men and women, one by one, into the fellowship of the Church of Jesus Christ as baptized, reproducing, growing disciples, fully able to disciple others. We are not talking about a mere game or a sports victory, but about an achievement greater than any success the world could ever experience. No accomplishment could be more significant than this one. Each success in bringing someone to the Savior and assisting that individual to become a producer of disciples will bring a euphoric sense of joy and accomplishment and the development of these attitudes will greatly enhance that success. Even all of heaven rejoices when an individual becomes a believer.

4. "Blessed are they which do hunger and thirst after righteousness: for they shall be filled." (Matthew 5:6)

What does it mean to hunger and thirst after righteousness? The Bible defines several different types of righteousness. In Matthew 5:20 He speaks of the, 'righteousness of the scribes and Pharisees' which will get you absolutely nothing. In fact I would choose, as the key verse in Matthew to be 5:20. "Except your righteousness exceed the righteousness of the scribes and Pharisees, you will in no case enter into the kingdom of heaven."

Then there is the "Righteousness of God" (II Corinthians 5:21) without which none of us will ever see God. God requires perfection and because we are not even close to being perfect, He gifts to us His own righteousness, made available by His grace, paid for on the cross by the blood of Christ and applied to us by our faith in Jesus alone (Ephesians 2:8). In His righteousness and in His righteousness alone, we stand justified (Just as if I'd never sinned) before God, our sins washed away by His blood for all eternity.

But the righteousness Jesus speaks of here is a righteousness which will enable us to be more and more effective in attaining our goal; that of reaching a lost world for Christ and assisting them to become a reproducing part of His Church. Jesus set an example for us according to I Peter 2:21, "...that we should follow in His steps." Jesus tells His disciples in Matthew 5:48 to be perfect, even as God in heaven is perfect. We will never be perfect in this life and thank God we do not have to be perfect because we are covered by His righteousness. But in order to accomplish the task of building His Church, we need to strive to be as righteous as He is righteous. How do we do that?

By being as hungry and by being as thirsty for a knowledge of God the Father and God the Son and God the Holy Spirit as we possibly can. Paul said in Philippians 3:10, "That I may <u>know</u> Him, and the power of His resurrection, and the fellowship of His suffering, being made conformable unto His death..." How do we find out about God? By reading and studying God's Word, the Bible. The more you know about God's Word, the more you will know about God!

The admonition in this attitude is to hunger after His righteousness. Have you ever been hungry? If you live in the United States, the chances are that you have never experienced real hunger. Most Christians in this country, unless they have fasted for forty days, have no idea what it means to be hungry. Job said in Job 23:12, "...I esteem His words more than my necessary food." We need to be hungry for the Word of God and to crave its message even more than we hunger and crave our physical food.

But Jesus goes on; we also need to thirst after the Word. Thirst is an even greater drive than hunger. You can be without food for as many as forty days and still be alive, but without water, death will overtake you in only a few short days depending on the conditions around you. We should thirst after His Word. Remember Paul's words in Philippians. "That I May <u>KNOW</u> Him!" Why is it so important to '<u>KNOW HIM</u>?' Because the more we know Him, the more effective we will be when introducing Him to others, to people who really need Him. The more we know Him the easier it will be to develop the attitude of humility, the more we know him the easier it will be to develop the proper attitude toward sin, to genuinely hate it, and the more we know Him the easier it will be to develop the attitude of meekness and put anger behind us. The better we know Him the more people who need the hope Jesus offers will be drawn to us so that we can introduce them to their Savior.

JESUS SAID THAT TO BE ALL THAT YOU CAN BE, TO BE AN EFFECTIVE DISCIPLE, YOU MUST HUNGER AND THIRST AFTER RIGHTEOUSNESS.

5. "Blessed are the merciful: for they shall obtain mercy." (Matthew 5:7)

All of us want others to act mercifully toward us, but we are so often reticent to show that same mercy toward others. Here Jesus is telling His disciples (and us) that if we want people to show us mercy, we need to be merciful.

His somewhat hidden message is even stronger; it is that if you are to maximize your effectiveness in reaching lost people for Christ, you must possess the attitude of mercy. Someone once defined 'grace' as something we are going to receive that we do not deserve, but 'mercy' refers to something we are not going to get that we rightly deserve. Eternal life is God's gracious gift to us, a gift we do not deserve, while we will not spend eternity in hell, a fate we rightly have earned.

God has shown to every believer incredible mercy and he wants us to show the same mercy to lost people. Genuine humility, a hatred for sin, a meek spirit and a hunger and thirst for righteousness will be a great help in developing this attitude. A mother, whose son was on death row, went to the Governor of the state where her son was in prison and asked him to show her son mercy. The Governor looked at her and said that her son did not deserve mercy. The mother's answer to the Governor was that if her son deserved mercy, it would not be mercy.

All of us have heard the expression, "There, but for the grace of God, go I." Each of us must constantly remind ourselves that because of our sin nature, we have the capability of doing some awful deeds and it is by the grace of God alone that we have not found ourselves doing them. I believe that even when non-believers make right decisions; it is by the grace of God. When we recognize our own faults and weaknesses our attitudes toward the mistakes of others become much more merciful.

JESUS SAID THAT TO BE ALL THAT YOU CAN BE, TO BE AN EFFECTIVE DISCIPLE YOU MUST BE MERCIFUL.

6. "Blessed are the pure in heart: for they shall see God." (Matthew 5:8)

In this attitude, I believe that Jesus is talking about our motives. What you do is not nearly as important as why you are doing it. Why do you want to be involved in the building of the kingdom of God? Is it to look good in the sight of your pastor or other believers? Is it because you think that God will love you more if you bring others to Him? Is it because you think that it will insure your own eternal life? You should not be concerned about what others think about you; only about what God thinks about you and you must never forget that He loves you, unconditionally. You can do nothing to make God love you more, after all He laid down His life for your salvation: "Greater love hath no man than this; that a man lay down his life for his friend." There exists no greater love than that which God has for you! His love is everlasting! And as for your eternal life, it was fully paid for at Calvary; there is not one thing you can add to it; just receive it. It's a gift from God to you!

So then, what should be our motive for serving our Lord? It should be LOVE! "And now abides faith, hope, love; these three, but the greatest of these is LOVE" (I Corinthians 13:13)! Our most important motive is our love for God and the Lord Jesus Christ. Paul said, "For the love of Christ constrains us;" (II Corinthians 5:14). We are motivated to reach the lost because of God's great love for us and His love for us is what causes us to love Him. I John 4:19 reminds us that we love Him because He first loved us! The greater our love for Christ, the greater will be our motivation to reach the lost for eternity.

Our love for Christ, if it is real, will translate into a love for lost people. In Matthew 25:40 Jesus makes this statement: "In as much as ye have done it unto one of the least of these, my brethren, ye have done it unto me." If we fail to love those for whom Jesus bled and died, we fail to love Him! God's motive for dying for the sins of the world was love for that lost world (John 3:16). Our motive for building His Church by reaching out to lost people should be our love for them, a reflection of Christ's love for them.

JESUS SAID THAT TO BE ALL YOU CAN BE, TO BE AN EFFECTIVE DISCIPLE, YOU MUST HAVE RIGHT MOTIVES.

7. "Blessed are the peacemakers: for they shall be called the 'Children of God." (Matthew 5:9)

One of the passages we were encouraged to memorize during our youth was "The Sermon on the Mount" which refers to Matthew, chapters five through seven. Over the years my understanding of the word 'peacemakers' seemed unclear and as is often the case when we memorize scripture without pausing to meditate on it. I did not stop to ponder the meaning of the word. But later on, while developing a message on the nine beatitudes of Jesus, I was forced to study the meaning of the word in the context of Matthew five. What is Jesus referring to when he mentions people who are 'peacemakers?' He is not talking about people who set up peace talks between warring nations or even between families in conflict as noble as that may be. Instead He is referring to real peace, the peace that only Jesus gives.

<u>A peacemaker in this context is one who brings people to Christ</u>. He is one through whom others see the character of Christ and are drawn by the Holy Spirit to a personal relationship with the Savior. He is an individual we often refer to as a 'soul winner.' Proverbs 11:30 reminds us, "…he that wins souls is wise." Jesus said in John 14:27, while talking about the Holy Spirit He would send later and referring to Him as 'the Comforter' He says, "Peace I leave with you, My peace I give unto you: not as the world gives, give I unto you. Let not your heart be troubled, neither let it be afraid." Real peace can never be realized in its fullness outside of a personal relationship with Jesus Christ. Until a person knows for certain that his sin has been forgiven, washed away, removed as far away from him as the east is from the west to be remembered no more for all eternity by God the Father and the Lord Jesus Christ, he can never know the peace that only Jesus can give.

Introducing lost people to the living Christ has to be the most exciting experience in the world. Talk about euphoria, I believe that there is no experience on earth that comes close to that one. The Apostle Paul believed that bringing others to the Savior was even more fulfilling than his own conversion. In Romans he speaks of his own personal sorrow and his own heavy heart caused by the fact that his own people, the Jews had rejected the Gospel message. Then in verse three of chapter nine he says this, "For I could wish that myself were accursed from Christ for my brethren, my kinsmen according to the flesh..." If bringing the lost to Christ were not more exciting than one's own conversion, Paul could not have made that statement. Is your love for the lost that great? If it were, would that change your priorities? The good news for us and for Paul is that we cannot lay down our salvation so another can have eternal life. The Lord Jesus has already done all that needs to be done and we can add nothing to His perfect plan. But if that were our heart's focus, if that were our motive, what an incredible difference it would make in our lives and in the lives or many others.

Let's say that you introduce someone to Christ and continue to disciple him/her for a year or so until each of you can go out and reach another for the Savior and disciple that one and you continue to do this for ten years, and each one follows through for the ten years. In ten years you would have been instrumental in bringing one thousand-twenty-four people to Christ and in assisting them to become disciplers. In twenty years the count would be one million, forty-eight thousand, and five hundred-seventy-six and in thirty years we are looking at one billion, seventy-three million, seven hundred-forty-one thousand, and eight hundred-twenty-four. In just three more years you would have influenced eight billion-five-hundred-eighty-nine million, nine hundred-thirty-four thousand, five hundred-ninety-two. You say, "So what?" The so what is that the population of our world is about six billion and when we take the Kingdom of God to all people, Christ returns!

I know that these numbers can be earth shaking, but before you finish this book, I hope to show you a very practical way we can actually accomplish this feat with a simple, doable plan: a plan that requires prayer, consistency, the attitudes Christ is sharing with His disciples in this part of Matthew, and less than three hours of your time each week, not counting personal prayer and Bible study which I trust you are already doing.

Has it ever occurred to you as it did to me several years ago, that in heaven there are only two things we cannot do that we can do on the earth? One is to sin and the other is to introduce others to Christ and His wonderful plan of salvation. After we meet Christ, following our conversion, for which of these two reasons does God leave us on the earth? Is it that we might sin? Clearly, that is not the reason. You may think that we are left so that we can grow spiritually, to learn about God's Word, to grow in character, to learn to pray and many other growing experiences. But my contention is that everything we experience as growing believers, without exception, is to help us to become more effective in winning lost people to the Savior. Peacemakers are people who make peace by bringing lost people to the author of real peace, the living Christ.

JESUS SAID THAT TO BE ALL THAT YOU
CAN BE, TO BE AN EFFECTIVE DISCIPLE,
PEACEMAKING MUST BE AN INTEGRAL
PART OF YOUR EVERYDAY LIFE.

CHAPTER FOUR

SOME WILL BELIEVE THE LIES
THAT ARE BEING TOLD ABOUT YOU

**8. "Blessed are they which are persecuted for righteousness sake: for theirs is the Kingdom of Heaven."
(Matthew 5:10)**

These two final attitudes Jesus speaks about are two very difficult assignments. The first seven are not easy by any means and certainly require an immense amount of personal discipline and self control, but these last two are where a lot of well meaning sincere believers disembark the ship. You see, if we are serious about winning the world for Christ, if we mean business about reaching a lost world, we will suffer persecution, guaranteed! The Apostle Paul reminds Timothy in II Timothy 3:12, "Yea, all that will live godly in Christ Jesus will suffer persecution." In Mark 13:13 and again in Luke 21:7, Jesus talking to the disciples tells them this, "Ye shall be hated of all men for my name sake." The writer of Proverbs reminds us that, "...he that is upright in the way is abomination to the wicked," so by simply walking with the Lord, your life will be a rebuke to those committed to wickedness. They will not like you, but others, sensitive to the Spirit of God will be drawn to you and you will be able to offer them the free gift that God has given to you, eternal life through faith in Jesus Christ.

Jesus taught this lesson, in all probability, very early in His ministry and the disciples did not 'get it' right away. In fact, throughout their time with Jesus on earth they were quite slow to respond to His teaching. They argued over who should be first in Christ's Kingdom, they battled for the seat on His right hand, they went out to minister to the multitudes and failed to accomplish much, they attempted to heal people and failed, but after Pentecost, what a difference! In Acts, chapter five the disciples were taken captive and ordered not to speak in the name of Jesus and their response was that it was better to obey God than to obey man no matter what the cost. They were beaten and then released, and what did they do? They went on their way rejoicing that they were considered worthy to suffer shame for His name! In John chapter fifteen, beginning at verse seventeen, Jesus says this; "These things I command you, that you love one another. If the world hates you, ye know that it hated Me before it hated you. If you were of the world, the world would love its own: but because you are not of the world, but I have chosen you out of the world, therefore the world hates you.

Remember the word that I said unto you. The servant is not greater than his lord. If they have persecuted Me, they will also persecute you: if they have kept My sayings, they will keep yours also. But all these things will they do unto you for my names sake, because they know not Him that sent Me." Ah! There's the key. "They know not God." That's our task: to provide an opportunity for them to 'know Him'!

Sometimes this persecution will come from good people, even other Christians who are convicted because their level of commitment is not as deep as yours. This persecution is not the same as that spoken of in verse eleven of Matthew's Gospel.

As you learn, develop and put into practice genuine humility, a holy hatred of sin, a meek spirit, a hunger and thirst for holiness (righteousness), a merciful perspective toward others, right and pure motives and the skill of presenting God's free gift to those who are without it, many will be drawn to you. But others will resist you, make fun of you and even persecute you. But they are like those who crucified Christ; they do not realize what they were doing. Jesus said on the cross, "Father, forgive them, for they know not what they do."

JESUS SAID TO BE ALL THAT YOU CAN BE, TO BE AN EFFECTIVE DISCIPLE YOU MUST BE WILLING TO SUFFER PERSECUTION FOR RIGHTEOUSNESS SAKE.

9. "Blessed are you when men shall revile you, and persecute you, and shall say all manner of evil against you falsely for My sake: rejoice and be exceeding glad for great is your reward in Heaven, for so persecuted they the prophets which were before you." (Matthew 5:11)

This one sounds a lot like number eight, but it is in fact quite different. In number eight the persecution is a reaction to your life style, attitudes that impress but at the same time, because they remind people of their failures, cause them to be very uncomfortable when you are around. These persecutors, as previously mentioned, could even be from professing Christians, convicted by your level of commitment.

This persecution, on the other hand, comes as a result of people who just want you out of the way, who oppose you philosophically and who are committed to false ideas. The truth of your life simply flies in the face of all that they believe to be true. They tell lies about you, they bring false accusations, they attempt to demean you and lessen your credibility. And often they succeed. We see this happen a lot in the world of politics. Politicians campaign, not on the characteristics they possess that qualify them for the office, but constantly demean their opponent by telling lies, or half truths so that the public will focus on the negative instead of the positive. Unfortunately, it tends to work. Proverbs tells us that "...the simple believes every word" (Proverbs 14:15).

Much of the false accusations brought against you will also be believed by some. I cannot help but think of one politician during a debate with his opponent who was claiming to be quite religious, challenged him with the intent to expose his hypocrisy. "I'll bet you one hundred dollars that you do not even know the Lord's Prayer," he taunted. "I'll take that bet," was the reply. The money was given to the moderator to hold and the candidate who had been challenged began to recite: "Now I lay me down to sleep. I pray the Lord my soul to keep. If I should die before I wake, I pray the Lord my soul to take. Amen." His opponent said, "You win, I didn't think that you knew it!"

Sometimes politicians do not have a very good reputation and we often tend to be quite critical of them. Someone once said that ninety per-cent of the politicians were giving the rest of them a bad name, but wait! These are some of the lost people Jesus is asking us to love to the Savior. What would happen if those of us who professed to be followers of Christ prayed for these leaders and asked God to give to us a genuine love for them. In I Timothy 2:1 we are admonished by Paul to pray prayers of intercession, supplication and even give thanks for those who are our leaders. We are told to respect our leaders and that they have been placed in their positions of leadership by God according to Romans 13. As believers in and followers of Christ our focus should always be toward introducing the lost to Christ and doing all we can to provide for them an access to God's free gift. If that is our constant objective, many will eventually come to the Savior. Many of these political leaders are among those Christ has commissioned us to reach!

Is there anything we can do to combat false allegations which will come at us at times? Yes: but how?

1. Learn to love our enemies. (Matthew 5:43-48)

2. Recognize the truth of Romans 8:28.

3. In everything give thanks. (I Thessalonians 5:18)

(I am so glad that Romans does not say that all things are good for sometimes they are not, or in I Thessalonians that we must be thankful for everything. Though we may not be thankful for the event that happened, we can thank God for what we learned as a result of the experience. And even in tragedy, which God does not cause, still He can use it for His own purpose and for our benefit. In Psalm 76:10 we read, "Surely the wrath of men will praise You (the Lord): the remainder of wrath You will restrain." This verse says to me that God is love. A loving parent will not artificially remove the consequence of a bad decision his child makes, because he wants his child to learn and grow. Because of God's love for you and me, He allows us to experience the results of bad decisions we make. God is not the cause of the problem or the tragedy. Man, giving in to his sinful nature is the cause. Sometimes we get caught in a trap set by others and we pay a dear price. This verse in Psalms tells me that even though man may make a bad decision, God only allows us to experience the consequences if those consequences will accomplish His purpose in the world and benefit us or someone else.)

4. Ask God to teach us to be humble.

5. Learn to hate sin.

6. Develop the spirit of meekness.

7. Hunger and thirst for righteousness.

8. Develop the gift of mercy.

9. Make certain our motives are pure.

10. Learn to introduce people to Jesus.

You can now begin to see why it took the disciples the greater part of three years to allow these attitudes to become a working part of their lives. They watched their Master during His life. They witnessed His trial and His response to many false accusations, watched Him submit to leaders who were clearly wrong, saw Him nailed to a rugged cross, heard Him call for the forgiveness of those responsible for His suffering, bow His head in death, rise from the dead on the third day and ascend to His Father in heaven. After that they prayed for one-hundred and twenty days before they began to 'get it.' And at Pentecost, in the power of the Holy Spirit, it was clear that they had at last, 'gotten it'! But they were still adding to the Church (Acts 2:41). Jesus wants us and He has called us to be multipliers in His Church. This begins to happen in Acts 6:7. Addition is good and we must continue to do it, but multiplication is better. Real disciples multiply!

JESUS SAID THAT TO BE ALL THAT YOU CAN BE, TO BE AN EFFECTIVE DISCIPLE; YOU MUST BE READY FOR UNFAIR TREATMENT, ESPECIALLY WHEN IT COMES BECAUSE OF YOUR FAITHFULNESS TO THE LORD JESUS CHRIST.

As you grow in these attitudes, you will be able to live in such a way that those who know you, but do not know the Lord will come to know the Lord, because they know you!

A word of encouragement! Do not wait until these attitudes are fully developed to begin to share your faith with others. Begin right away. What you will discover is that as these attitudes grow in your life your effectiveness in introducing people to the Gospel will increase proportionally. The results will thrill you beyond your wildest imaginations.

CHAPTER FIVE

SALT AND LIGHT

Why does Jesus teach them concerning these nine attitudes? Why are they so important? He answers these questions in these next two verses, verses thirteen and fourteen. These attitudes are important because, number one, "You are the salt of the earth" and number two, "You are the light of the world." Let's look at salt first.

In verse thirteen of Matthew 5 Jesus states, "You are the salt of the earth: but if the salt has lost its savour, wherewith shall it be salted? It is thenceforth good for nothing, but to be cast out and trodden under foot of men." The word 'savour' in the old KJV refers to saltiness. If the salt is not salty, it is worthless; throw it away. Jesus is telling His Disciples that they are going to flavor the whole earth. And how are they going to do that? They will do it via their attitudes. Anger breeds anger, greed breeds greed, selfishness breeds selfishness, a love for sin encourages others to find themselves in its trap, but humility impresses, a hatred for sin along with a love for the sinner communicates to the sinner, meekness fends off anger, righteousness sets an example, mercy helps people to be open to counsel, proper motives foster trust and a knowledge of the plan of Salvation prepares you to bring peace to those who are ready to receive it. In other words, our saltiness is in our attitudes and that is why Jesus begins His discipleship training class with an emphasis on attitudes.

There are two positions of power in the world; that of authority and the other of influence. Which of the two do you think is more powerful? Influence is by far the greater power. An authority can demand certain behavior, but one with influence causes the one he is impacting to want to do the right thing. The authority needs a police force to make certain his orders are followed, but the one with influence need not worry because the desire to do right comes from within the individual who has responded to his influence. The more we learn these nine attitudes and put them into practice, the greater will be our ability to flavor (influence), to impact the earth for Christ.

Then Jesus goes on in verses fourteen through sixteen to talk about a disciple being the 'light of the world.' He says, "You are the light of the world. A city that is set on a hill cannot be hid.: neither do men light a candle and put it under a bushel, but on a candlestick; and it gives light unto all that are in the house. Let your light so shine before men that they may see your good works and glorify your Father which is in heaven." But in John eight, verse twelve, Jesus clearly states, "I am the light of the world." John chapter one also has much to say about the fact that Jesus is that light. Yet here in Matthew Jesus tells the disciples that they are the light of the world. What message is He conveying to them?

In our world the sun gives light during the daytime and also at night, but at night it requires the moon to reflect its light to the dark side of the earth. In the same way we as disciples are to be reflectors of the love of Christ to a dark and dying world. Jesus is the light of the world, but that light is reflected to the world through us. How do we reflect that light most effectively? We do it by developing the nine attitudes so vital in the life of an effective disciple. The more these nine attitudes are developed, the brighter our light and the saltier our salt. The more we master humility, a hatred of sin, a spirit of meekness, a holy lifestyle, a spirit of mercy, a pureness of motive and a knowledge of God's wonderful plan for our salvation, the greater will be our impact on the world and the more likely the people we influence will be to bring glory to God as a result of our witness as verse sixteen directs us.

In verses seventeen and eighteen Jesus presents an important truth which I am certain went right over the heads of the disciples the first time they heard it. Not until we read some of their writings later on do we know that they finally understood it. Jesus said, "Think not that I am come to destroy the law or the prophets. I am not come to destroy but to fulfill. For verily I say unto you, till heaven and earth pass, not one jot or one tittle shall pass from the law, till all is fulfilled."

This fulfillment, this satisfaction of the law, even to one 'jot' and 'tittle', was completed in the lifetime of the disciples. In fact they had only about three years to wait for its completion. The Bible reminds us that sin's wage is death and that there is no way that we can avoid sin's penalty or pay for our own breaking of the law (fulfilling the law of God in our own lives). Instead, Jesus on the cross, paid our penalty, thus satisfying the whole law even to every 'jot' and 'tittle' in our lives so that now we are totally justified through His blood (just as if I'd never sinned).

You see, to be a disciple, we must be as righteous as God, Himself. In ourselves that can never happen so God allows us to place our sin on Jesus and in its place He gives to us His own righteousness which is perfect and pure. II Corinthians 5:21 tell us this: "For He (God) hath made him (Jesus) to be sin for us, who knew no sin, that we might be made the <u>righteousness of God</u> in Him!" This is the good news our Lord is preparing us to share with lost people. This is the good news that will change their lives on the earth and insure an eternity with their Creator. This is why heaven rejoices every time someone comes to Christ (Luke 15:7, 10). This is why we need to keep as our main focus in life, amid all the other good and important tasks that lie ahead, the command from our Master to influence people in this dark world to call on the name of the Lord. Once this is done, we must help them to become men and women who can reach and encourage others to do the same.

Now Jesus continues with verses nineteen and twenty of Matthew five. Verse nineteen says, "Whosoever, therefore, shall break one of these least commandments and shall teach men so, shall be called least in the Kingdom of Heaven, but whosoever shall do and teach them, the same shall be called great in the Kingdom of Heaven." The cost of our salvation is completely paid for in the death, burial and resurrection of the Lord Jesus Christ so why the admonition to do and teach His commands? Because our goal is to reach a lost, dark world for Christ and to do this we must 'hunger and thirst after righteousness.' When we enter fellowship with Christ at conversion, we become 'new creatures' in Christ (II Corinthians 5:17). Our old life passes away and our focus becomes new.

The believer does not keep the commandments to be saved or to stay saved; he keeps them because his new nature causes him to want to live in obedience to Christ. The love of Christ constrains him (II Corinthians 5:14) and he also understands that in order to be most effective in accomplishing God's task for him in this world, he must live in obedience to his Savior. I cannot help but believe that our greatest joy in eternity is going to be the occasions when we meet people who are alive because we were where God could use us as instruments to bring them to Christ. Even more exciting will be the knowledge that He used that individual to bring another person to Christ to many generations. Discipleship is where the action is! But to be at maximum effectiveness we need the right attitudes.

In fact the next verse in Matthew five, verse twenty is a clear warning from Christ to His followers: "For I say unto you, that except your righteousness shall exceed the righteousness of the scribes and Pharisees, ye shall in no case enter into the kingdom of heaven." Let's look at the righteousness of the scribes and Pharisees for a minute. What do you see? What about humility, their attitude toward sin (visible in their hatred of sinners) their lack of meekness, their lack of mercy, their selfish motives and their rejection of Christ. These attitudes are absolutely unacceptable in a true disciple. We will see more of these comparisons as we continue through the book of Matthew and we will examine that comparison in ensuing chapters.

Are you beginning to see the importance of the word 'attitude' in the successful completion of that which Christ has called us to accomplish? The discipleship process must include the discussion, evaluation and working together for the purpose of developing these attitudes in ourselves and in each other.

CHAPTER SIX

YOU HAVE HEARD...BUT I SAY

As Jesus continues on in chapter five of Matthew, He uses three illustrations of how these nine attitudes will affect the disciple's response. He begins verses twenty-one, twenty-seven, thirty-one, thirty-three, thirty-eight and forty-three with the phrase, "You have heard that it has been said, but I say unto you." In other words, this is what you have grown up believing, it's what you have been taught, but to be effective in reaching a lost world for the Kingdom, I'm telling you to let these nine attitudes alter your approach to these situations.

'You have heard that killing is wrong, but I am telling you that to be bent out of shape is wrong, for anger is what leads to killing. If someone is upset with you, don't respond in anger, practice the spirit of meekness, go and make things right and do this even before you worship. You will avoid many costly consequences by responding with the attitudes I am speaking about, and are more likely to experience success in reaching a lost world for Me.'

Jesus continues; 'you have heard that adultery is wrong, but I'm telling you that even the lustful thought you entertain when looking at a woman is adultery in your heart.' Proverbs 23:7 tells us that as we think in our hearts, so are we.

Thoughts lead to actions, actions lead to habits and habits lead to addictions.

In verses 29 and 30 Jesus is encouraging us to hate sin! He tells us that sin is so destructive that it is better to lose an eye or a hand than to let it entrap us in its clutches. Don't even think about sin. Remember Paul's admonition: what we allow our minds and our members to become involved in will eventually lead us to that which we will serve. Let sin reign and we will serve sin. Let righteousness rule and we will serve righteousness. Jesus is saying, "Sin; don't even think about it!"

In verses 31 and 32 Jesus focuses for just a moment on marriage, for their law permitted divorce for almost any reason and sometimes for no reason at all. A disciple, to disciple at maximum effectiveness, must have the right relationship with his/her spouse. Paul points this out to Timothy in I Timothy 3:5 when he tells him the importance of having things right at home in order to be successful working in the Church. This does not disqualify those with problems at home, but may make it just a little more difficult.

So to divorce your spouse for any reason except fornication is to cause her/him to commit adultery. The only reason Jesus says 'except for fornication' in this passage is that if fornication is the reason for the divorce, he/she is not causing the spouse to commit adultery, adultery has already been committed. I do not believe that this is the exception clause as so many are prone to teach.

In verses 33 through 37 Jesus points out their tendency to stretch the truth at times. Instead say, "Yes" or say, "No" and mean what you say. Be honest in your dealings with people and you will win their trust. These nine attitudes will help you in this endeavor.

Verses 38 through 43 have been taken out of context by many unbelievers to promote a cultural myth. Jesus is addressing His disciples, not nations. It is the task of disciples, not nations, to make disciples. Jesus says to His disciples, you have been taught that you get even, that you punish those who offend you, but I am telling you to turn the other cheek, go the second mile and when someone steals from you, give them even more than they took in the first place. Boy, do we ever need these nine attitudes to accomplish these tasks! Remember, our ultimate goal is to win lost people to Christ so it stands to reason that those who offend us are a part of the lost world we are called to reach. Good things happen when we do things God's way.

A young boy, about twelve years old, was playing one day near his home in Jerusalem when a Roman Centurion came toward him. The Jews hated the Romans for the Romans held them in bondage and this lad dreaded what he feared was about to happen. His first impulse was to run and hide, but if he were caught he would be flogged, so he just waited and the thing that he feared came to pass. The Centurion called to him roughly and demanded, "Hey kid, carry my pack!"

Now the Roman law required a Jewish boy to carry the pack one mile, not a step more. So the lad took the pack and with disgust, began that mile. As he walked he remembered that just a few days before he had heard a man outside of Jerusalem, on a hillside say, "If someone makes you go a mile, go two." "How dumb," he thought, "why would I want to do that; it makes no sense?" But the more he walked, the more he thought about it and as he neared the end of the mile he decided that he would just try it.

At the end of the mile, as the Centurion reached for the pack, the lad said, "Begging your pardon, sir, but with your permission I would like to carry this pack another mile."

"Say what?' was the startled reply. "You want to do what?"

"I'd like to go another mile with you," was the reply. The surprised Centurion agreed and they began the second mile. As they began walking, the Roman soldier looked down and asked, "What's your name?" He told him.

"What's yours," the young man asked in return? He told him.

Before long the Centurion was telling stories of life in the army, what it was like inside the Palace. He told of interesting experiences while on guard duty with the King, and the conversation was so enthralling that before the lad knew it, the second mile was completed. The soldier reached down for his pack and thanked the boy, encouraging him to hurry home; his mother would be worried.

"Could I come and visit you sometime, he asked? I would like to meet your family."

"Just think!" the lad thought as he headed home. He now knew a Roman Centurion by name and had enjoyed a lot of his personal stories about life in the Roman service. What had happened that day? In the first mile, he discharged his responsibility, but in the second, he made a friend.

Another story I remember hearing at the "Institute in Basic Youth Conflicts" by Bill Gothard, concerned two young Christian farmers in the Orient working all day to fill their rice field with water. To do this they had to carry the water from the pond to their field by hand. After a long hard day's work and a good night's sleep, they discovered, as they went out the next morning, that their neighbor, during the night had gone out, dug a ditch between their field and his and drained all the water from their field into his field. They were a little upset, but being believers in Christ, they chose to forgive their neighbor and spent another day filling their field.

The next morning they discovered that it had happened again. In fact it happened four days in a row and they found themselves disliking this neighbor more than a little bit. They became bitter toward their neighbor so they went to talk to their Pastor about the situation and about what they could do to get rid of their bitterness toward this neighbor.

The counsel that he gave shocked them. He told them, "Tomorrow, when you carry water up the hill, don't put it in your field, put it in your neighbor's field." "You have got to be kidding," was their startled reply. "This guy has already stolen four days work and now we are to work for him even more?" The Pastor looked at them with great empathy, telling them if they could not do it he would understand, but they had asked him how they could get rid of their bitterness, and that would do it if they meant business.

On the way home they decided to try it, even though it made no sense. So the next day they worked till noon filling their neighbor's field and finished it with the help of the last four days of work and the rest of the day put the water in their own field.

When their neighbor went out that evening to steal again, he realized what they had done and was blown away. The Holy Spirit began to convict him and several days later he came to their home, knocked on the door and said, "I do not understand. Why did you do what you did for me when I wronged you?"

They were able to tell him of their relationship with the living Christ and that because of their love for Christ, they loved him and chose to interpret his actions to represent a need in his life that they might be able to fill. As they told him of the Savior's love for him, he wanted to know more and not long afterward they were able to introduce him to Jesus Christ.

Jesus said that if someone takes your coat; give him your cloak also. When these attitudes become a part of our personalities, incredible miracles will happen. Any time someone embraces the Savior and is given eternal life, it's a miracle!

Jesus is speaking to His disciples in this passage in Matthew, chapter six, He is not addressing nations. In government it is still, "An eye for an eye and a tooth for a tooth." The world is not under grace, only the believers. It is not the disciple's responsibility to punish wrong doing, but it is the responsibility of the government to do so. The Bible teaches that when an individual purposely takes the life of another, he must die. This is still true. In Romans 13:3 and following we are told that rulers (governments) are not a terror to good works, but to evil. Our leaders are ministers of God to help us do good, but if we choose to do evil, be afraid, "...for he bears not the sword in vain." What is a sword used for? It does not lock and unlock prison doors. It is an instrument of death. Because this principle has not been applied to the world, our world has become a much less safe place in which to live and will become even more so in the future, but not to worry. Governments will ultimately be required to answer to God for their failures: this responsibility is their responsibility. Ours is to win the lost for Christ and to help them become soul winners and disciples.

Jesus said that they had been taught to love their neighbor and hate their enemies. "If you are going to be successful in building My Church, this must change. You must learn to love your enemies. Bless them, pray for them, do nice things for them and even love them." Why should you do this? Because you are God's child and your enemies are potential children of God: lost people for whom Christ died! Therefore the nine attitudes must come through in our everyday living and the more they do the more effective we will be in reaching others for Christ.

This portion of His message is wrapped up with the words, "Be ye therefore perfect, even as your Father in heaven is perfect." Jesus knows that everyone who places his faith in the Lord Jesus Christ is made perfect at conversion because he is given the very righteousness of God (II Corinthians 5:21). But in order to attain maximum effectiveness as a disciple, we must work to become more and more like Christ in our everyday lives. Will we ever attain perfection in this life in the flesh? No, we won't, but the more we become like Christ the greater the impact our lives will have on others.

And how do we become like Him? We do it through a study of the Word, through prayer and by fully surrendering our lives to Him in such a way that these nine attitudes become a part of our everyday lives. It is a process. It does not happen all at once. Even the disciples slipped once in a while, even after Pentecost.

Why not ask God to make you salt and light: to teach you these nine attitudes so that you can be even more effective in the Holy Spirit's desire to use you in reaching the world for Christ?

CHAPTER SEVEN

THE SCRIBES AND PHARISEES
ARE BAD EXAMPLES

As Jesus begins what is to be one of His most earth shaking sermons in chapter five of Matthew, He clearly outlines His nine focal points right at the beginning and then He illustrates them throughout the rest of His message. One of His main concerns is that disciples, His disciples, never adopt the attitudes of the scribes and Pharisees, who were the religious leaders of His day (Matthew 5:20). So now as we continue on to chapter six of Matthew we hear Him expanding on this theme.

When you give to God, don't give as the scribes and Pharisees give. They like to give out in the open to impress others with their generosity; they have all the reward they're going to get. God is not impressed! And when they pray, they want to pray out in the open, even in the street to be seen of others. They will receive no more than that from their prayer life. God is not impressed! And when they fast, they make it obvious to others that they are fasting so that others will admire then for their piety, but guess what? Again, God is not impressed and their fasting accomplishes nothing more than the feeding of their own egos.

Jesus points out the importance of tempering our giving, praying fasting and everything else we do in our obedience and worship of Him, with these nine attitudes. When you are genuinely humble, when you hate sin realizing the devastation that it leaves in its wake, when you are concerned about the rights of others rather than your own rights, when you want the Holy Spirit to totally control your life, when your hatred of sin causes you to look mercifully on the weaknesses of others, when your motives are to please only God and no one else, when you realize that you have the words of eternal life to offer to lost people and that these lost individuals matter a lot to God, when you are so focused on your task that opposition, rather than slowing you down, spurs you on in your commitment to proclaim His name and when strong opposition from people trying to break you, doing whatever it takes to derail you, even telling lies in convincing ways about you, so that many believe the lies: when you experience all this and it <u>motivates</u> rather than discourages you to continue to do what God has called you to do in spite of the cost, you will find your self giving, praying fasting and everything else you do for Christ falling directly in line with His instruction on how these things should be done.

In reading chapter six in Matthew, verses 9 through 15, it seems at first, that our Lord may be 'chasing rabbits'. What is meant by the term, 'chasing rabbits'? On occasion a pastor right in the middle of his message will go off on a tangent, sharing an idea that is not in his notes and not even thought about during his preparation time, and at times the tangent that he is on has little to do with his overall message. Sometimes it can be a good thing brought about by the Holy Spirit, but often it is the result of his pet peeve or personal interest and can even become a detour from that which God is trying to convey through his message. Most of us as pastors have been guilty of this on more than one occasion.

When Jesus is speaking about 'when you pray', He inserts information on how to pray and the importance of forgiving others. I do not believe that He is guilty of 'chasing a rabbit.' He is, instead answering a question.

Other writers record that the disciples at one time asked Him, "Lord, teach us to pray!" Jesus did what a good teacher almost always does; He answers the question right away. As you set up your discipleship groups of four that we will discuss in a later chapter, when a question is asked, stop the discussion and focus on the question. To put it off to a later time in the session or even to the next session could greatly reduce the impact the discussion will have on the questioner. For the most effective learning we try to get the student to focus on the subject and the question reveals that the focus is already there. Take advantage of the opportunity! What a great example of good teaching here is afforded by our Savior.

When the Lord allowed us to pastor a Church in the Baptist General Conference for a few years, I remember an expression often shared with us as pastors by our Executive Minister over the Eastern region. He reminded us again and again; "Remember to always make sure to keep the main thing the main thing." This is the focus of Jesus for the remainder of the chapter. His message is, 'do not be distracted! Keep the main thing the main thing.' Your focus is not earthly riches, it is eternal riches. You cannot serve self and God at the same time. It will not work! The main goal is not meeting everyday needs, it is to be seeking first the Kingdom of God and His righteousness. When that is your priority, everything else falls into place. At the very end of the Book of Matthew, after Jesus gives His great commission, He promises, "Lo, I am with you always, even unto the end of the world," (Matthew 28:20) a reinforcement of verses 25 to 34 of this chapter in Matthew.

Continuing on into chapter seven, we again read warnings from our teacher to avoid the practices of the scribes and Pharisees. He warns us not to criticize others, but rather to take a long look at ourselves. A realistic look at one's self tends to temper how we look at others. Remember how the rulers brought a woman taken in the very act of adultery to Jesus asking Him to pronounce judgment? The response of our Lord was that since stoning was the penalty in the law for such an offense, the one present who was without sin would throw the first one. As Jesus wrote in the sand the people who had been so critical, now began to leave, one by one. By the way, the law required that both the man and the woman be stoned. Where was the man in this picture? The hypocrite will not be very effective in winning the lost to Christ. Remember the nine attitudes and learn how to make them a part of your life.

In verse six of Matthew seven we are reminded that everyone with whom we share this wonderful free gift of salvation will not respond kindly to our efforts; not to worry! Our message is precious and very valuable; we are not to waste it on scoffers.

In verses seven through eleven Jesus encourages them to trust Him for their needs and to never be afraid to cry out to God in prayer. His admonition is to ask (pray), seek (go look for it), and then act on it (go get it). God cares for us even more than our earthly fathers.

The well known verse twelve can only be consistently followed if the nine attitudes are an active part of the believer's life. "As you would that men should do to you, do you even so to them, for this is the law and the prophets." In verses thirteen and fourteen He emphatically points out that there is only one way to eternal life and only a few will find it (but still our goal is to preach the gospel to every creature as noted in Mark 16:15), He warns them to look out for false prophets and shows them how to identify them, and then He clarifies the true believer in twenty-one to twenty-three. Professing to know the Lord with no lifestyle to back it up is evidence of a false prophet. But at the same time, many wonderful works done in the name of Christ, done in order to impress others is also a sign of the same thing. Let me attempt to explain.

There is only one way to God and eternal life: that is through believing in Christ and Christ alone. Works contribute nothing to your salvation. In Ephesians 2:8 & 9 we read, "For by grace ye are saved through faith; and that not of yourselves, it is the gift of God: not of works lest any man should boast." When this takes place in the life of an individual, a miracle happens! He is reborn (John 3:3, 5), He who had been dead has been brought to life (Ephesians 2:1) and he has become a new creature in Christ (II Corinthians 5:17). Everything changes; sometimes instantaneously and sometimes it takes a little time to actually see the change, but there is always change.

We looked at Ephesians 2:8 & 9, but let's go on to verse ten: "For we are His workmanship, created in Christ Jesus unto good works, which God hath before ordained that we should walk in them." The supernatural result of a person coming into a real relationship with the Lord is a desire to walk with Him and to be obedient to His leading. If one professes to know Him and this desire is not there, it would be a good time to follow the Apostle Paul's admonition in II Corinthians 13:5 to, "Examine yourselves, whether ye be in the faith; prove your own selves, know ye not how that Jesus Christ is in you, except ye be reprobates (counterfeits, false prophets)." The Word of God clearly teaches us that we can 'know that we have eternal life' (I John 5:13), but a sense of security can be eternally fatal if it is a false sense of security, so we need to be certain. James put it this way: "...Show me your faith without your works and I will show you my faith by my works (James 2:18)." Remember Christ's words, "By their fruits you shall know them" (7:20).

Now Jesus concludes His message with an illustration. Many preachers who come to their pulpits as pure teachers (the gift of teaching as the motivating gift from the Holy

Spirit), feel that illustrations are a waste of time in any sermon, because their goal is to disseminate information, so they proceed to bore their congregations to death (except for those in the crowd who possess the same gift) with their barrage of information which often flies over the heads of most of the people. I remember Pastor Smith who was a marvelous Bible teacher and was invited by my father to come on the staff of the Federated Church in East Springfield, Pennsylvania. When he preached he was anything but boring and I held on to every word, but he would poke light fun at my dad because he would use a number of illustrations in his messages. But when he saw how the people responded to Dad's sermons, he began to use them in his messages and the result was that an already impacting message became life changing, increasing his effectiveness many times over.

Was Jesus a teacher? Of course He was, but He was also the Holy Spirit so He possessed all the gifts of the Spirit. And now He drives His message home with an illustration: the wise man builds on rock, but the foolish on the sand. As He brings this discourse to a close, we understand that we need to seek wisdom and to build on the 'Rock' (Jesus Christ), not the 'sand.' How do we accomplish this? By obedience to Him!

It was hard to keep the multitudes away from Him so as He taught His disciples, they began to edge closer and closer and at the end many were listening. And their conclusion was that, "This man knows what He is talking about! He really makes sense!" Is He making sense to you? Be sure to read

Matthew as you read through this book, for there is important information that I'm certain will not be discussed in this writing. We are building blocks in Christ's Church. How do we most effectively build on the Rock, Christ Jesus? By growing in grace and allowing the Holy Spirit to develop these nine attitudes into our very being. A fitting way to close this chapter is to note the Centurion Jesus meets in Capernaum, who requests that Jesus heal his servant. The servant was a man the Centurion cared for deeply. When Jesus offers to go to his home, the man hesitates for all the right reasons. He is a centurion and yet he demonstrates several of these nine attitudes, the most notable being humility as he feels he is not worthy of having a man of Jesus' stature in his home. Jesus' response is very revealing. He tells His disciples and the multitudes around Him that this Roman Centurion has shown more faith than anyone, so far, in all Israel. What was it that Jesus saw in this man? Attitudes can make a powerful difference in our failures and in our successes.

CHAPTER EIGHT

WITH THE RIGHT STRATEGY, YOU CAN REACH THE WORLD IN ONE GENERATION

We jump now to the end of chapter nine of Matthew's gospel, for remember we are looking at Matthew from the standpoint of discipleship training. Beginning at verse thirty-six we read these words: "But when He (Jesus) saw the multitudes, He was moved with compassion on them, because they fainted and were scattered abroad as sheep having no shepherd. Then He said to His disciples, 'The harvest is plenteous, but the laborers are few. Pray to the Lord of the harvest that He would send forth laborers into His harvest.'" Here, again, we see the love Jesus has for the multitudes and therefore the necessity for disciples. He urges them to pray for harvesters knowing full well that they would, at least in part, answer that prayer. You are the answer to the rest of the prayer!

The world will never be won for Christ through addition. Success in fulfilling the great commission requires multiplication. In Acts, chapter two, verses 41 and 47 we are told of the growth of the Church through addition. But in Acts six, verse seven, after a change in attitude toward some very special people in the Church, we find the church multiplying! What is the difference? As we discuss this difference, please note that there is nothing wrong with adding to the Church. We need to keep doing this, but we will never reach the whole world until we work on multiplication.

Let me illustrate: if an evangelist preached every day for fifty years and saw two-thousand people accept Christ every day he would, during his lifetime, reach thirty-six million, five-hundred-twenty-five thousand individuals. We would give God praise and glory for each of these, but that computes to slightly more than six tenths of one percent of the world's population, not counting the additional births during those years. That's addition. 36,525,000 souls won to Christ is incredible, and we are excited about each of them, but we have hardly scratched the surface in relation to the whole world. What the Church has accomplished over the past one hundred years is mostly the result of addition, with an occasional multiplication thrown in. In the early fifties approximately seventy-five percent of the population of the United States attended church at least once a month and now that figure has dropped to less than twenty percent. We need to multiply!

Another illustration: suppose you promise yourself and the Lord that you will reach ten people for Christ every day of your life for seventy years. You are not going to bed any day until you know you have led ten people to Christ. If you could do this and if you were successful, you would reach in your lifetime two-hundred-fifty-five thousand, six hundred seventy-five people. Again, praise the Lord for each of them, but in relation to the whole world into which we have been commanded to go, we have reached about .0043 percent (forty-three ten thousandths of one percent) of the world's population, again not taking into account the individuals born during those seventy years. So how many of you will commit, right now, to refuse to sleep any given day until you have led ten people to the Lord? Why not? Because you say that in the first place it cannot be done and in the second place, even if it could be done we have accomplished very little in relation to the whole world which, by the way, was the focus of our Lord, and you would be right!

So, what is multiplication and how does it compare to addition? Paul, in his second letter to Timothy, chapter two, verses one and two writes, "Now, therefore, my son, be strong in the grace that is in Christ Jesus and the things that thou hast heard of me among many witnesses, the same commit thou to faithful men who shall be able to teach others also." In other words, making disciples happens when we are successful at teaching people to teach people to teach. When you introduce someone to Christ, you have added one to the church, but when you work with that one until he/she is able to lead others to Christ and assist the new converts to do the same, you are multiplying and who knows the number who will be reached as the result? Addition to the Kingdom often results in instant gratification (which we Americans crave), but multiplication requires patience and time; lots of time. My goal in this chapter is to help you catch the vision as to what you could accomplish over time if you are consistent and obedient to Christ's call upon your life through multiplication.

Going back to our previous illustration of addition, we are pretty certain that reaching ten a day, every day for seventy years, or even one year for that matter, is virtually impossible and incredibly impractical. But could you commit to giving an average of one to two hours every week for the purpose of investing time in the life of one person for six months to a year and then do it again with someone else? Is this scenario possible? Yes! It is extremely doable!

Let's see what might happen. You work with one person, meeting together, praying together in a study of the basic tenants of the faith, and at the end of the year there are two people ready to reach one and disciple that one. Now you both do this same thing with someone else and after two years there are four ready to go out. After three years there are eight disciples, after four years sixteen and after five years there are thirty-two.

By the way, this is precisely why we do not do this. Five years have passed and we have only thirty-two to show for it, and that is only if all carried through which some probably will not. But watch what happens over the next five years.

Years	Disciples
6	64
7	128
8	256
9	512
10	1024

Pastors go to seminary and then spend fifteen or twenty years building a church of one thousand, or five hundred or even smaller and you, without seminary training have potentially impacted more than one thousand people for Christ and they are not just believers, but they are disciple multipliers. Let's keep going with this illustration and let's see what happens over the next few years.

Years	Disciples
11	2,048
12	4,096
13	8,192
14	16,384
15	32,768
16	65,536
17	131,072
18	262,144
19	524,288
20	1,048,576
21	2,096,152
22	4,194,304
23	8,388,608
24	16,777,216
25	33,554,432
26	67,108,864
27	134,217,728
28	268,435,456
29	536,870,912
30	1,073,741,824
31	2,147,483,648
32	4,294,967,296
33	8,589,934,592

Now we have a problem. In thirty-three years we have potentially reached eight-billion, five-hundred-eighty-nine million, nine-hundred-thirty-four thousand, five-hundred-ninety-two people, <u>BUT</u> there are only approximately six billion people living on the earth. We have run out of people! In other words, mathematically speaking we could reach the whole world in thirty-three years or less: that's one generation, and we can accomplish this if we are willing to invest approximately one to two hours a week in an individual for six months to a year.

By the way, I need to explain that the ideas in this book were given to me by the Holy Spirit, via many men and women who were faithful to God's call and under whom I have had the privilege of studying. If you read an idea in this manuscript that you shared with me: that's probably where I learned it. Thank you for your faithfulness.

Now let me give to you an approach to this principle of discipleship that could work. The last part of this idea was given to me by my son's (Tim) family's pastor of the Church of the Nazarene in Ashland City, Tennessee, Pastor Charles Gates, as I was sharing this vision with him.

Let's assume you have just led someone into a personal relationship with Christ. What happens next?

Step one is to schedule one hour a week, for several weeks in order to help the new believer in Christ to begin to understand what has happened to him/her. In another chapter I will share with you the material I use and let you know where you can get it, but there are a number of organizations that have good material and you need to find the material that you can use comfortably (this part of the plan came to me via a fellow pastor who now pastors a church in Randolph, New York, Pastor Allen Jones).

Next put together a group of three (four including you) for the purpose of working together to learn to reach and disciple others. Where can you find the other two for your group? Look for two zealous believers, who have perhaps been walking with the Lord for years, but have not yet caught the vision of multiplication, or on occasion another new convert with a desire to grow. Ask the seasoned believers if they would assist you in discipling the new convert. Investing your life in only one for a year could be discouraging if at the end of that year he chooses not to continue. But with four of you working together, the chances of at least one going on with you are pretty good and with all four working together, encouraging each other, the probability of all of you going forward is a good possibility.

Don't worry about the six billion people in the world; focus on your group. Be consistent. Be faithful. Trust God for the results. Some will fall by the wayside, but that is not your problem, it is God's problem. If you faithfully invest those few minutes each week, in ten years, in twenty years, in thirty years, hundreds of thousands will have been brought to the Savior, most of whom you will never know. But remember, God is the score keeper. He knows and cares for each one.

Every decision for Christ results in a party in heaven and God will credit your account with every believer on whose life you had an influence, even if that influence was through someone else that was impacted by someone else, who was impacted by someone else, who was impacted by you.

Pastor Marlin Mull, Pastor of the Wesleyan Church located in the Wesleyan Village in Brooksville, Florida, brought a message one July Sunday morning about Gad, one of Jacob's sons. As the brothers gathered with their dying father who was giving a blessing to each of his sons, this is what he said in his blessing to Gad: "Gad, a troop shall overcome him, but he shall overcome at the last." A Warning: trouble ahead! The challenge: don't quit! The victory: you will win! As you form your groups there is a warning, this is not going to be a piece of cake; there is trouble ahead. You will experience times of discouragement. If you do not, something is wrong. Something this effective will not be ignored by the enemy. In everything give thanks! Never quit, be faithful and trust God for the results, "…In due season we will reap if we faint not." (Galatians 6:9) The victory! Another building block in the Church that Jesus is building with the potential for a lot more. Gad's victory is seen in Revelation 7:5, "…of the tribe of Gad were sealed twelve-thousand."

One additional thought: if you implement this plan and carry it out without any attrition (and there will be attrition) you will reach the world in thirty-three years. If two begin, we cut that figure to thirty-two years. If four begin and carry it through we cut the years to thirty- one. How about a thousand-twenty-four believers begin today, without attrition, we can reach the world for Christ in twenty-three years. How many believers are there in the world today? What if one million believers began this process today? We could reach the world for Christ in just thirteen to sixteen years, even with attrition. Are you willing to be one of them?

Your victory will be a little visible here and now, but the real celebration for you will be in eternity when the Lord shows you the fruits of your faithfulness. "Thank you for giving to the Lord. I am a life that was changed! Thank you for giving to the Lord: I am so glad you gave!"

CHAPTER NINE

FOCUS ON THOSE WHO ARE
OPEN TO YOUR MESSAGE

As we open chapter ten of Matthew we find Jesus setting up the disciple's internship portion of their training. They still have not been elevated to full discipleship status, but Jesus sends them out on a practice mission to help prepare them for their ministry after Pentecost. We have no record of their successes or failures during this time of training, but we can glean some information from our Lord's teaching that will help us once we are out in the field of battle.

His initial instruction is to go only to the house of Israel; do not go to the Gentiles. This affirms Paul's admonition in Romans, chapter one when he says that he has a debt to all men, but to the Jew first (Romans 1:16)! In our outreach to the world we should always be praying for the Jewish people because they are special to our heavenly Father. Even after the Nation of Israel had rejected Jesus again and again, still each Israelite has a very special place in the heart of God. Among the saddest words in the Bible are the ones found in John 1:12. "He came unto His own and His own received Him not..." Still Jesus makes Israel a priority and we should, too.

He empowered them for their assignment and tells them not to take a lot of baggage with them; God will provide. Our focus should be on the needs of the lost, not on our own needs. They are to minister to those who are open and walk away from those who are not. The key here is that we are not to argue or fight. We plant the seed and if it is rejected, leave and go to others more open to the message. Who knows but what someone who today is closed to the message might, at a later time, become open to it.

From verse sixteen of this tenth chapter of Matthew, Jesus prepares them for the difficult times ahead. Most of the difficulties about which He is speaking would come after Pentecost, but the nine attitudes He spoke about in Matthew five would be essential for success on this mission and for those in the future, especially numbers eight and nine, but all come into play.

He encourages them: He says that they should not fear; God will take care of them, even if the worst happens (Matthew 10:28). He tells them not to be afraid, even if they are facing death; God is in charge. You are valuable to Him; He knows what you need. Your focus is to confess Jesus before men and women, boys and girls, no matter what the cost.

Next He talks about priorities. "I must be first in your life; ahead of mother, father, son, or daughter," He admonishes them, "even if as a result they turn against you, still I must be first." Some of you who have sat under our ministry in the past are thinking, "Does this fit in with the priorities you used to teach us?" And the answer is, "Yes, in every way." Those priorities were; God first, family second (Spouse and children in that order), ministry third (ministry includes your job) and self last.

Paul reminded Timothy in his first letter to him that to be at the peak of effectiveness in the Church, he must be an effective leader at home. If he does not have a right relationship with his wife and family, how can he expect to handle the problems at the church (I Timothy 3:5)? But what Jesus is communicating in Matthew 10 is an admonition to 'keep the main thing the main thing.' They were never to forget why they were disciples. What is the number one goal? It is to reach and disciple the world to Christ, one at a time. Do not turn to the right or to the left; let nothing deter you from your mission. Note verse thirty-eight of Matthew ten and following: "And he that takes not his cross, and follows after Me, is not worthy of Me. He that findeth his life shall lose it: and he that loseth his life for My sake shall find it."

And what is necessary to accomplish this? Prayer, the right attitudes, a deep, deep love for Christ, proper care for the family, a desire to please Him in all you do, a willingness to be inconvenienced for the sake of our Lord and for the people He has sent you to reach, and one to two hours of your time each week. Keep in mind that there is nothing that you will ever do in life that is more important than bringing an individual to Christ, and then investing yourself in him/her for six months to a year until he can reach and teach someone else. There is a chorus we used to sing in Sunday School that went like this: "With eternity's values in view, Lord, with eternity's values in view; may I do each day's work for Jesus with eternity's values in view." Never forget that our life is not about today and tomorrow as important as that may be, but it is about eternity and the difference between life and death for people who desperately need a Savior, most of whom are completely unaware of their need for Him. Think about it! We can do this in the power of God's Holy Spirit.

Jesus concludes this portion of the training with a promise; no matter how small any action you may take might appear you will not go unrewarded: even a cup of cold water given to a child in the name of a disciple will be rewarded. Your living will not be in vain.

In chapter eleven, beginning with verse twenty, Jesus foretells a curse on those cities that reject His teaching and the ministry of the disciples. He says, "Woe, unto thee, Chorazin! Woe unto thee, Bethsiada! For if the mighty works, which were done in you, had been done in Tyre and Sidon at the day of judgment, they would have repented long ago in sackcloth and ashes...It shall be more tolerable for Tyre and Sidon at the day of judgment than for you." And He goes on to talk of Capernaum.

As you purpose to share Christ, some will respond with great enthusiasm, but others will reject you and your message. This passage reminds us of Paul's words in Romans twelve when he writes, "Vengeance is mine, I will repay, sayeth the Lord." The knowledge of this truth frees us to love those who oppose us, knowing that God will deal with our offenders. Remember, if you hit those you resent with a hammer, you are going to jail. But if God hits them with a hammer, they can't do anything about it and God has a bigger hammer. Also, keep in mind that when you take vengeance or react to an offense, your purpose is to get even: but when God takes vengeance on your behalf, He does it to bring those who offended you to repentance and isn't that why we spoke to them in the first place? This requires the attitude of 'meekness'

Chapter eleven concludes with these well known words: "Come unto Me, all you who labor and are heavy laden, and I will give you rest. Take My yoke upon you and learn of Me, for I am meek and lowly in heart and ye shall find rest unto your souls, for My yoke is easy and My burden is light." Living for Christ, sharing the gospel with lost people does not have to be a chore. God wants us to enjoy His creation, to care for our loved ones, to encourage each other in our walk with Him. Laying aside one to two hours every week can accomplish much over time as we diligently use those minutes, plan for those minutes, pray over those minutes, allowing God to use us as a channel through whom He can reach the whole world for Himself. With the help of Almighty God, we can do this! Just be consistent and faithful: work and enjoy all that God is doing in your life. Remember, there are 168 hours in a week and if we tithe our time, we owe God 16 hours and 48 minutes and of course you want to offer Him a little more (tithes and offerings) which will still leave you more than 145 hours every week to do other things that you enjoy and need to do.

CHAPTER TEN

TAKE UP YOUR CROSS, MY BURDEN IS LIGHT

In this manuscript, I am attempting to look at the teachings of Jesus that He directed to His disciples, but there are other principles they learned as they walked with Him and watched. At the end of chapter twelve of Matthew's gospel, His mother and His brothers come looking for Him and He offers His well known reply, but little understood statement, "Who is my mother? And who are my brothers?" Then looking at His disciples He said, "Behold my mother and my brethren! For whosoever shall do the will of My Father which is in heaven, the same is my brother, my sister and my mother."

A true disciple does the will of the Father and it need not be burdensome. "My yoke is easy and My burden is light," were Jesus' words in Matthew eleven. We are saved by God's grace, grace entered into by faith in Jesus alone (Ephesians 2:8 & 9), but look at verse ten of Ephesians 2: "For we are His workmanship, created in Christ Jesus unto good works, which God hath before ordained that we should walk in them."

Remember, there are two things and only two that we can do on earth that we cannot do in heaven. The first is sin; and the second is to be used of God to win the lost to Jesus Christ.

Everything else that we do here, we can do there. For which of these two purposes do you suppose God leaves us here on earth after we are saved? The answer is obvious! Jesus tells us at the end of chapter twelve of Matthew that true disciples accomplish His will: they reach the lost (II Peter 3:9).

In chapter thirteen of Matthew, Jesus speaks in parables to the multitudes, but He explains them to His disciples. The first is about sowing and reaping. Paul, in Galatians 6:7 and following reminds us that what we sow, we reap. If we sow to satisfy ourselves, we will reap corruption, but if we sow that which is of the Holy Spirit, we will reap life everlasting!

Jesus tells the multitude that a farmer went out to plant (sow) seed and some fell on stony ground, some fell on shallow ground, some fell where thorns and weeds were present in abundance and still some fell on good ground, grew up and produced a lot of fruit.

Later the disciples came and asked why He spoke in parables? His reply was that the multitude was not yet ready to understand the mysteries of the Kingdom of Heaven. He would teach His disciples the mysteries and then, when they were ready, they would teach the rest of the world. 'As yet, the masses are not ready to hear, but your eyes are open and you are ready to listen,' He tells them, 'so I will explain the story to you.'

He explains that the seed that they plant goes out to the masses and will fall on four types of ground. The first is rock; the second is thin, the third falls among thorns and the fourth on good soil.

The rock represents those who hear, but do not understand and before they have a chance to think it through, satan comes and devours the seed and takes it out of reach. The thin soil represents those who hear and receive the word with joy, but soon their enthusiasm fades away and they are no different than before. The third are those who at first seem to make sense of the Gospel message, but are later overcome by the cares of this life and of the flesh and as a result abandon their walk with Jesus. The second and third appeared to trust in Christ, but did it for the wrong reason and did not actually put their trust in Christ, therefore when the pressure came it was easy to walk away. Salvation comes when we place our whole trust in Jesus; when we realize that He has paid it all and by faith we rest in Him alone. Only what we share in Him matters.

The people in the thin soil and in the thorny soil, while appearing to be saved, never grasped the real meaning of God's grace and therefore never really knew Him or experienced saving grace. (Now don't abandon me here. I believe that there will be Calvinists and Armenians in glory so if you see this in a little different light, don't quit; keep going! Whatever your theology, the result is the same. We all agree that they are lost.)

The fourth soil is good ground and these are the ones who understand the plan of salvation by grace and are regenerated by the blood of Christ. These bring forth much fruit; some by the hundreds, others by sixties and others by thirties, but all multiply. It is interesting to note that if over the span of your life here on earth you reach and disciple just thirty-three people who will in turn do the same, you will reach the world in a generation.

Jesus shares another parable in verses 24 through 30. He tells them that as they build His Church, the enemy will creep in and these bad plants (tares) will grow right along with the good seed and sometimes it's hard to tell which is which. Jesus warns us to be careful! Sometimes when attempting to get rid of the 'tares' you hurt the good seed. Focus on reaching the lost. God and His angels will separate the good from the bad in the time of harvest (Matthew 25:31-46).

In verses 31 and 32 Christ likens the Kingdom of heaven to a grain of mustard seed, a very small seed, and one you can hardly see when it stands by itself and yet it grows into the largest tree in the forest and many are comforted by it. People outside the faith often benefit when Christians are being salt and light. The tree provides shade, moisture and a place for birds to rest in its branches.

What I believe He is telling them (and us) is that no matter how small or unimportant our sharing of the gospel might seem, when sown faithfully and with the right attitude, it will result in great dividends for the Kingdom of God. The beauty of multiplication is that while you are concentrating on a few, they will also reach a few who will reach a few until multitudes are reached for Christ and much of this will happen without your knowledge. You know that you are doing what Jesus has commanded you to do and the rest is up to Him. "One plants, one waters, but God gives the increase."

Verse 33 of Matthew thirteen gives us another illustration of the Kingdom of God. A little leaven, placed in the dough, impacts the whole loaf. As we are faithful in living the nine attitudes of chapter 5, disciples will impact the whole world and influence even those who do not embrace the plan of salvation; the whole world around us will be affected. The Gospel is so powerful, that when properly proclaimed by true disciples, everyone will respond to it in some way. Some will respect believers without becoming one of us, others will be angered by our lives and our commitment, and thank God some will embrace our Savior as their Savior, but all will feel its impact.

In verses 37-43 of Matthew, chapter thirteen Jesus explains the parable of the tares to His disciples. In the parable of the soils the seed was the Word of God and disciples are the ones that sow the seed, but in this story Jesus is the one who sows, disciples are the seeds, the field is the world, the tares are the children of satan planted by the devil, the harvest is the end of the world and the reapers are the angels. In the harvest two crops are gathered: Those that offend and promote sin and iniquity are gathered and cast into the furnace and are burned and the description Jesus uses is wailing and gnashing of teeth. The other crop consists of the children of the Kingdom who allowed Jesus to pay for their sin and are covered by His blood and righteousness. They shine forth as the sun in the Father's Kingdom for all eternity. The description of the lake of fire in Scripture should be ample motivation in and of itself for believers to want to share the Gospel message with the lost although there are many more good reasons to do so. Of course the best reason is the fact that Jesus commanded us to do it (Matthew 28:18-20, Mark 16:15, Luke 24:46-48 and Acts 1:8).

Let me share a thought that might encourage you during times when you feel that your effort to reach an individual for Christ is going nowhere. The tares that are planted by the devil will probably never turn to Christ and are unreachable, so no effort will succeed in bringing them to Christ. The problem for us is that it is difficult if not impossible for us to tell the difference between the tares and the wheat. That is why Jesus tells us to let them grow together and the Angels will solve the problem at the harvest. We need to treat everyone as a person for whom Christ died and pray for them, but do not lose sleep if they do not respond (unless prompted by the Holy Spirit to stay up and pray), for it is God and God alone who can bring them to Himself. We are only the conduit through which Christ's power flows that allows us to <u>bear</u> fruit, only Christ can produce the fruit (note chapter seventeen in this book).

In verses 44-46 of Mathew, chapter thirteen we find two more illustrations of the Kingdom of God. A field that contains great treasure and a pearl that is priceless. When the pearl and the treasure are discovered, everything is sold in order to amass enough money to purchase them. There is no price too great, even if I have to give up everything I own, I must possess the pearl or the field. Why? It is because all my needs will be met by owning the field or the pearl. Everything I gave up will be replaced by my new wealth. That's how valuable it is to know Christ. He has all power in heaven and in earth: He owns the cattle on a thousand hills, everything belongs to Him and a personal relationship with Jesus Christ makes you His child and His heir. What more could you want?

Be careful not to interpret this parable as paying for your salvation. That is a free gift, it costs you nothing, but there is a responsibility of ownership. Perhaps this illustration will help. Just suppose that I want to give you a gift, so I take on a second job and work from six until midnight, six days a week for ten years, placing all my earning from that job into a savings account until I have enough money to buy and pay for a brand new Rolls Royce with all the bells and whistles. After making the purchase, I drive to your house, knock on your door and present my gift to you completely paid for and delivered to your driveway. I present this new car, my gift to you. I have worked for the money, purchased the car, delivered the car to you and presented my gift. Now it is your turn to respond.

There are at the least, three possible responses. The first is that after hearing of what I did to provide this car for you, the investment of a significant part of the last ten years of my life, you might feel blown away by my effort and so you say to me, "Wayne, that is an awesome gift, I am blown away by it and never in a thousand years did I know that I meant so much to you. But it is not fair to you to have had to pay the whole price by yourself: here, let me help. Here's twenty dollars to help cover the price of the car. You have just insulted my gift and me! I paid upwards of $150,000 for your gift and you are going to help me pay for it with a twenty dollar bill? That is exactly what we do to God when we acknowledge that Christ died on the cross for our redemption, but we feel we need to change, or go to church, or do good deeds, or help earn this incredible gift some other way. The gift of eternal life was paid for by the blood of the Lord Jesus Christ and to offer or attempt to earn it is to insult the God of heaven. He paid the full price and offers the gift to us because of His love for us and to the awesome price He paid we can add nothing!

The second response you can make when the car is presented to you is to acknowledge that you are grateful for the thought and for my effort, but you say, "Thanks, but no thanks, I do not want the responsibility of owning a six figure automobile. I do not want to pay for the insurance, I am afraid of repair costs when something goes bad. I just do not want a $150,000 car in my driveway!"

You see, while salvation is a free gift, given by God, there is a responsibility of ownership and many who are confronted with the Gospel just do not want to pay the price of ownership. If you refuse my gift, it cannot be yours. To own the gift, you must receive the gift. It does not matter that I bought the car for you. It does not matter that I love you. It does not matter that your name is engraved on the glove compartment. If you do not receive my gift, it is still mine.

In Matthew 16:24, Jesus said, "If any man will come after Me, let him deny himself, and take up his cross and follow Me…" But remember, He also said, "My yoke is easy and My burden is light." Yes, there is a price of ownership when you come to Christ: not to be saved or even to stay saved, but because you are saved! But with God's grace, we can accomplish everything that He calls us to do.

The third response you could make to my gift is this: "Wow! Wayne, you mean you invested a significant part of your time over the last ten years, so that I could own this car? I don't know what to say! I did not know that you loved me that much. I want to thank you for your gift, I am accepting it because I believe (by faith) that it is paid for and I am not going to be stuck with the bill. You will know how much I appreciate what you have done for me by how I treat your gift. I am going to wash it every day, wax it once a week, build a garage to keep it in when it is not being driven and in the winter I will put it up on blocks to protect it from the salt. Believe me, where ever I go driving this car, I am going to tell the people I meet about you, my special friend, who sacrificed so much to make this gift possible. A lot of people are going to hear about you and your generosity!

This is the response God wants from us when He offers His gift of salvation to us. "Heavenly Father, You paid an awesome price for my salvation and I receive it by faith, knowing that what You paid was enough. From now on, as I live for you, sheltered in the garment of your love, I will share with all who will listen, the wonderful grace of Jesus that is also available to them. Because of your love for me, I will live my life in obedience to You!

In verses 47-51 of Matthew , chapter thirteen Jesus uses yet another illustration that they will be more apt to understand, because many of them were fishermen. He refers to a fishing net, full of all kinds of fish, some edible and some worthless. The two are separated, saving the good fish and throwing the bad away. Again He refers to the furnace of fire for the wicked where there is wailing and gnashing of teeth. This is an important concept for them to grasp evidently, for Jesus mentions it several times and in verse 51 asks them, "Do you understand?" So we must ask ourselves as this chapter of the book comes to a close, "Do we understand the importance of the Kingdom of Heaven?" The more we understand, the greater will be our motivation to share this wonderful message and gift God has given to us and to others.

CHAPTER ELEVEN

COMBAT FALSE TEACHING WITH
THE TRUTH OF GOD'S WORD

In Matthew, chapters 14 and 15, we again see Christ's incredible love for the multitudes as He feeds them in the wilderness. Even though they follow Him everywhere, He knows His only hope to make them an eternal part of His Church requires the training of His disciples so that they can train other disciples. Addition is good, but addition will not get the job done: we need to multiply! His motive for training these men is His love for all men and women. He meets their physical needs in the present, but for eternal dividends, He needs disciples.

In Matthew 14:25-33, a famous event occurred known to most people across the world. It was an important experience in the training of the disciples. Jesus is walking on the water toward the ship and His presence strikes fear in the twelve. Jesus assures them that there is no need to fear with the words, "Do not be afraid! It is I."

Peter's response is, if it is You, Lord, tell me to come to you on the water?" Jesus said, "Come on!" In an incredible demonstration of faith, Peter begins to walk on the water, but when he takes his eyes off Jesus and looks around at the boisterous sea, he doubts and begins to sink. In great fear he cries out, "Lord, save me!" Immediately Jesus was there, caught him by the hand and brought him to the ship. This was a teaching moment for Jesus so He says to Peter, "Why did you doubt? What happened to your faith?"

Upon reaching the boat, the disciples worshiped Him and affirmed that they were convinced that He was the Son of God. If we are going to be effective reaching people for Christ, we must be absolutely certain that Jesus is who He said He is, God manifested in the flesh (I Timothy 3:16). Notice that the disciples, upon seeing Jesus walking on water, <u>WORSHIPED HIM</u>. Jesus did not object. The angel in Revelation vehemently objected when John tried to worship him (Revelation 22:8 & 9). This is clear evidence among many others in Scripture, that Jesus is in fact God manifest in the flesh. In the Old Testament God declares that He will not share His glory with another (Isaiah 48:11), yet He shares it with Jesus. Why? Because Jesus is God! It is next to impossible to introduce Christ to lost people if we do not know His actual identity.

As we read on in chapter 15 of Matthew's Gospel we find the Pharisees and scribes complaining because the disciples did not always wash their hands before eating bread. Jesus challenges their theology, but does not challenge their position as leaders. These Pharisees and scribes are tares in all probability, but to question their position would cause unnecessary conflict, so He does not do it. That's what He said in 13:30 of Matthew's Gospel: "Let them grow together and the angels will handle the problem at the harvest."

In this instance Jesus does not attack these probable tares personally; He simply declares the truth in contrast to what they were teaching. This is how we should handle false teachers. Simply proclaim the truth of God's Word. Scripture tells us that, "Ye shall know the truth, and the truth shall make you free" (John 8:32). Reject false teaching and combat it with the truth and let God deal with the false teacher. <u>NEVER ARGUE!</u> You seldom win an argument and on the few occasions when you do win, you only cause your opponent to dig into his false teaching more deeply and then he becomes even more entrenched in believing his lie. Instead, simply plant seeds of God's truth and God's Word will never return to you void. When there is no argument, the individual is more apt to contemplate the truth that you shared and the Holy Spirit is able to make the seeds grow in his heart.

In verses 12 to 14 of Matthew fifteen the disciples noted that Jesus, while challenging the theology of these false teachers, had offended these religious leaders. They saw an illustration of Jesus teaching about the tares. The plants not planted by God will eventually be rooted out, so "Let them alone." They are blind leading the blind and they, along with their followers, will eventually fall into a ditch.

The enemy loves it when we get caught up in fighting the tares; that's one reason he plants them: to divert our attention from our main mission which is reaching lost people for Christ. Later, Jesus does attack these false teachers directly, but He is God so He knows their true identity: we can only guess so we leave the task to the Angels.

It is a sad thing that over the past one hundred years many giants in the faith have spent endless hours attacking men and women they were convinced were not of God and in retrospect we now know that some of them were of God. Jesus told His disciples when they told Him they had rebuked someone for teaching in His name, "He that is with Me cannot be against Me." How much more effective would it have been had they proclaimed the truth of God's Word and focused on reaching a lost world for Christ. In some instances they actually, unwittingly blocked the work and ministry of the Holy Spirit as He worked through God's anointed who was preaching the Gospel of Christ. Remember; always keep the main thing the main thing!

In verse 15 of Matthew fifteen, Peter asks about the parable in verse 11. Jesus explains that it is not what goes into the mouth that defiles us, but what comes out that is the problem. When evil thoughts, murders, adulteries, fornications, thefts, false witness, blasphemies come out of the mouth, and I am certain that this is not the complete list: when these things come out of the mouth, these defile the man.

Again, we must reflect back to the nine attitudes in Matthew, chapter five. This might be a good time to go back to chapters 2, 3 & 4 of this book and go over them again. If these attitudes are a consistent part of your life, out of your heart will come good things, not evil. This will make you a more effective disciple. Don't worry about what goes in: let the Holy Spirit control what comes out.

About eleven years ago I met a man in Clearwater, Florida when I answered an ad in the paper for an automobile. I did not buy the car, but the two of us became fast friends. This was God's appointment. This man did not know the Lord and in every paragraph he spoke the "F" word was used two or three times. He knew that I was a pastor so he apologized over and over again, but it had become a habit, and habits are hard to break. I reasoned that if I focused on helping him to get over using that word, he would go to hell with a clean mouth, so I refused to react when the word was used.

About one year into our friendship, one day after having lunch, I asked him if I could share something with him that had changed my life and he agreed. After telling him about Christ and His incredible plan of salvation, I asked him if he would like to acknowledge Jesus as his own personal Savior. I assured him that our friendship would continue if he chose not to pray the sinner's prayer and even encouraged him not to accept Christ if his only motive was to please me. Our relationship would not change.

He chose that day to open his heart to Christ and we prayed together behind my car by the side of the road. You know what? Old habits are hard to break, but over the next several months I heard that word less and less and in the last seven years he lived, I never heard it at all. You see, the Holy Spirit, as he grew in the Lord, took that particular expression away from him with no help from me except our friendship. Shortly after his conversion he found the Moody Radio

Network in Florida and listened to it constantly while growing in grace.

After he found the Lord, he would call me every three or four months to encourage me in my ministry. What a blessing he was to me. Not too long ago I was invited by his family to conduct his memorial service in Port Richey, Florida. There I had the opportunity to share his testimony with his family and friends. Christ has not called us to condemn the lost, or change the lost, or battle the lost, but He has called us to witness to the lost. He wants us to be a channel through whom He can love lost people and bring them to Himself and then disciple them through us so that they will be able to reach others for Him.

In verse 6 of chapter 16 of Matthew Jesus says, "Take heed and beware of the leaven of the Pharisees and of the Sadducees." The disciples misunderstood thinking that Jesus was complaining because they had nothing to eat and when Jesus perceived their thoughts He said, "Hello! Don't you remember what just happened? Multitudes were fed out of nothing!" Then they understood that He was warning them to be aware of the false teaching of their religious leaders.

To get caught up in false teaching will undermine the goal Jesus has put forth for us which is to reach the lost for Him. How can you identify false teaching? Study the Bible. Know God's Word! Weigh every new thought against the barometer of the Holy Scriptures.

When the FBI trains its people to deal with counterfeit money, they are never shown counterfeit money. Instead they study real money and become thoroughly familiar with it. Then when they come across a counterfeit bill they recognize it right away because they know the real thing. The more you study God's Word, the less apt you are to ever be deceived by those who falsely represent it.

In verses 13 to 20 of Matthew sixteen Jesus wants to make His true identity very clear to the disciples. His first question is, "Who do others say that I am?" Then He asks, "But whom do you say that I am?" Then He hears from Peter what is often referred to as Peter's great confession: "You are the Christ, the Son of the living God!" Jesus praises him calling him blessed and assuring him that the Holy Spirit had just spoken through him.

Jesus goes on to say, "You are Peter (a little stone), and upon this Rock I will build My Church and the gates of hell will not prevail against it." Some have used this passage to teach that Christ is building His Church on Peter. Not so! What is the subject of this paragraph? It is Jesus! "Who do men say that I, the Son of Man am? But who do you say that I am?" So when Jesus says, "You are Peter, and on this Rock (subject Jesus Christ) I will build My church," He is referring to the Son of Man (Himself), not Peter.

For clarification we need only to go to Peter's first epistle, chapter two, verses 4 through 8. "To whom coming as a living stone, disallowed indeed of men, but chosen of God, and precious…" Jesus was the one disallowed by men, not Peter. Jesus was crucified for our sins, not Peter. He goes on: "To whom coming as unto a living stone (Peter), are built up a spiritual house (the Church)" Verse six: "…Behold I lay in Zion a chief corner stone, elect, precious: and he that believeth on Him shall not be confounded." This corner stone on which Peter tells us the Church is built is clearly Christ, not Peter. We do not believe on Peter for our redemption: we believe on Christ! To believers, this stone is precious, but to unbelievers it becomes a stumbling block and an offense. In verse nine Peter writes: "…that ye should show forth the praises of Him who hath called you out of darkness into His marvelous light." He does not write, that you should show forth my praises who has called you out of darkness into my marvelous light.

In verse 19 of Matthew, chapter sixteen Jesus is simply saying to Peter and to the rest of His disciples that they are going to be the ones to whom He will give the power and authority to build His Church. He finishes this discourse by telling them not to reveal to the masses His true identity: not yet! Timing is everything.

Pray when you share your faith. Seek the timing of the Holy Spirit. There is a time to speak and a time to keep silent. I was Bob's friend for about a year before it was time to tell him about his Savior. When I shared, he was ready and open.

Then Jesus begins to tell them of the incredible price He would have to pay in order to redeem mankind. Peter objects and believing that he was doing the right thing, pledged to fight to the death to save Jesus. Then Jesus said to Peter, who moments before had spoken by the Holy Spirit, "Get thee behind Me, satan: thou art an offense unto Me: for thou savourest not the things that be of God, but those that be of men." Notice how easy it is to be speaking truth one moment and heresy the next. We need to know God's word as thoroughly as possible in order to avoid this trap (II Timothy 2:15, 3:16 & 17).

This chapter of Matthew concludes with the cost of discipleship. Verse 24: "If any man will come after Me, let him deny himself, take up his cross and follow Me. For whosoever will save his life shall lose it: and whosoever will lose his life for My sake shall find it." When you give Christ all that there is of you, He more often than not returns most of what you have given back to you. Now what you have is sanctified and fit for the Master's use. Now it can be used to accomplish your goal of reaching lost people for Him. Remember His promise: "Seek ye first the Kingdom of God and His righteousness and all these things shall be added unto you." (6:33) and again in Matthew 11:28 to 30: "Come unto Me, all ye that labor and are heavy laden and I will give you rest...FOR MY YOKE IS EASY AND MY BURDEN IS LIGHT."

I remember reading years ago about a missionary from China who was walking with a friend across the icy cold snow covered mountains. Tired, spent and beginning to get sleepy, they looked and saw the lights of the village far below, still a good distance away. The cold was already making them sleepy and it was questionable that they could even make it to their destination before the frigid air would overcome them. As they started toward the lights, they came to a mound of snow and after looking more closely, found the body of a man, fallen from the cold. After an even closer look, it was determined that the man was still alive. The missionary asked his friend to help him carry the man to the village.

"Are you crazy," came the reply? "We will barely make it ourselves. If we allow this man to slow us down, we are dead for sure!" Then he went on alone.

The missionary could not leave the man to die, so he bent down and with what seemed to be his last ounce of strength, hoisted the man over his shoulders and began his descent to the village. And then a strange thing happened. The effort that it took to carry the stranger caused the blood to surge through the veins of the missionary and this gave him new strength. As they neared the village, the motion of the walk aroused the stranger and he was able to walk the rest of the way under his own power. But as they neared the village, they found another mound of snow and as they brushed the snow aside, they found the body of the friend, frozen to death: the friend who had said, "If you want to lose your life trying to help this stranger, go ahead. I'm going to save mine." This is what Jesus is talking about in chapter 16. The more you surrender to Him, the more living you will experience. It is one of the great mysteries of the Gospel. No one has ever lost anything by giving his all to the Savior!

CHAPTER TWELVE

JESUS LOVES AND PROTECTS
THE LITTLE CHILDREN

In chapter 17 Matthew relates the event known to us as the transfiguration of Jesus, an event neither he (Matthew) nor any of the other disciples with the exception of Peter, James and John, were aware of until after Jesus had risen from the dead. There were a number of experiences in the life of Christ that God ordered to establish firmly in the minds of the disciples and us that Jesus was the manifestation of God in the world and this was one of the major ones. When Peter attempts to say something significant during the experience, God Himself, in a very nice way, tells him to be quiet and learn from His Master, the Lord Jesus. As at the baptism of Jesus, the voice of God again declares that Jesus is the Son of God! Remember, if we are to proclaim Christ to the world, we must know who He is in reality.

The transfiguration experience triggered a question after the four of them came down from the mountain and the question was this: "Why do the Scribes say that Elias must come before the Messiah?" Jesus assures them that he had already come: that the prophecy of Malachi 4:5 & 6 was fulfilled in part in the life of John the Baptist, again helping them to further understand who He was.

Later in chapter 17 we find a man who brings his son to the disciples for healing and they cannot do it. When Jesus learns of their failure, He seems a little upset and possibly a little frustrated. This is for our benefit for there are times in our working with new believers that we are going to be discouraged and even want to quit, but Jesus, though often experiencing difficulty, stayed with them to the end, even after their bitter failures during His experience at Calvary. Are you not overjoyed that He did not give up on them, for if He had, none of us would know Him and the hope we have in Christ would be non existent. Remember the words of Jesus recorded in Luke 9:62: "No man, having put his hand to the plough, and looking back, is fit for the Kingdom."

After Jesus casts out the demon from the lunatic son, the disciples asked Him, "Why couldn't we do that?" Notice His answer: "Because you have no faith!" His actual words were, "Because of your unbelief!" In verse 17 He uses the word, 'faithless.' Jesus does not say that they did not have enough faith. He said they had <u>No Faith</u>. We often hear people say that they need more faith, or that they lack an amount of faith. That is not possible. You either have faith or you do not. You either believe or you do not! Jesus, Himself uses the expression, "O ye of little faith" several times, but in the context He is simply stating their lack of faith.

In this passage, He goes on to say that if you have the faith equivalent to a grain of mustard seed, it is enough to move mountains. Evidently, a little faith is all you need. Having faith is like being pregnant. You cannot be a little bit pregnant. You either are or you are not. Faith is the same: you either have it or you do not. If you believe, you believe. If you believe, you act on that belief. As we share with a lost world this greatest story ever told, we must be absolutely convinced that Jesus is everything He claimed to be and that He alone is the answer to man's dilemma, Christ is the answer! Someone once said, mockingly, "If Christ is the answer, what is the question?" It does not matter what the question is, Christ is the answer to every question in some way, shape, or form. People need Him and we can help meet that need. Are you ready? Can you invest the equivalent of one to two hours a week in order to help win the world in a generation? I can hear the voice of Jesus now saying to you in glory, "Well done, good and faithful servant."

At the end of chapter 17, Jesus shows us an important principle of discipleship. Should we pay taxes to a godless government? Jesus did. What is the lesson for us? Our main purpose is not to change the government, nor is it to make our lives more comfortable. Our purpose is to win the world for Christ. Let's always remember to keep the main thing the main thing. Because of the way our republic is set up in the United States, we have an obligation to vote, to influence for right, to take a stand on important issues, but our energies are to be focused on that lost person God has brought into our lives or that new believer we are in the process of helping to become a new disciple. Refusing to pay tax to a government that will grossly misuse it will only result in unnecessary interference in the more important work of introducing people to their Savior. Pay the tax!

As we continue into chapter 18 of this Gospel of Matthew, the importance of the attitudes of chapter five again come into play. It is obvious that the disciples have not yet plugged into them. "Who is greatest in the Kingdom of Heaven" was the question? Jesus takes a child on His knee and tells them that unless they are like this child, they cannot even enter into the Kingdom. Children were considered unimportant in Jesus' day and yet the greatest in heaven would be those who were humble, who hated sin, those who had no rights, who were pure, who were merciful, those who had pure motives, and those who had simple childlike faith in Jesus: these who were like children would be the greatest in His Kingdom.

He goes on to say that His Father loves these new believers, that He will protect these young ones and that to offend even one of them would carry horrible consequences. These would be offended, and necessarily so, but judgment is waiting for the one who carries out the offense. Handle these new believers with care, for in heaven their angels behold the face of the Father. As we read this passage, it would seem that Jesus is talking about literal children and I think that is in the passage, but I believe that the meaning goes beyond the child to the babe in Christ. Those we work with are tremendously important to God.

In verse 11 of Matthew eighteen Jesus reminds us that the reason He came into the world was to win the lost, and that is also why we exist as believers in Christ, to win the lost. Paul tells us in Ephesians 6:12 that we are in a battle, not against flesh and blood, but against spiritual wickedness in high places. Do you think that satan is happy about your resolve to win the world for Christ in a generation? Of course not, so there are going to be spiritual battles, battles we cannot win alone.

In verse twenty of Matthew's gospel Jesus encourages us to band together for fellowship and prayer. Pray about people you are going to witness to and hopefully win to Christ. He promises that if two agree touching any one thing, God will do it! It is vital that in the process of this adventure that you stay in fellowship with a church and under the authority of godly leaders. You also need a place to bring the new believers into fellowship with others so that they can experience the help of others as they grow in the Lord.

In verse 21 of Matthew eighteen and following, Peter asks a question of the Master about forgiveness. "How often do I need to forgive a brother who offends me: seven times?" Peter thought he was being magnanimous. Jesus response shocked him: "Not seven times, but seventy times seven." Jesus is not suggesting that after four hundred-ninety times forgiving your offender you can now retaliate. Real forgiveness requires forgetting the offense. If you forget, you do not remember: if you do not remember, you cannot keep score. Therefore you will never reach four hundred-ninety.

Among the many things God taught me while attending the "Institute in Basic Youth Conflicts Seminars, advanced seminars and pastor's seminars, was a definition of forgiveness which I have shared many times with congregations and with myself when I need to be reminded. Here it is! "Forgiveness is healing others, by using their offense as an opportunity to express to them, Christ's love." Isn't that good? Read it again: "Forgiveness is healing others by using their offense as an opportunity to express to them, Christ's love." Read that over and over again. When it clicks, you will find yourself looking forward to people offending you so that you will have the opportunity to show them Christ in you, the hope of glory. The nine attitudes of chapter five will greatly enhance your ability to do this.

This is Jesus' message throughout the rest of chapter eighteen.

CHAPTER THIRTEEN

THE MOST IMPORTANT THING
YOU WILL EVER DO

In the beginning of chapter 19 Jesus deals with marriage, divorce and remarriage. This passage, in my opinion, has been grossly misinterpreted by many well meaning Christian teachers, but we are not going to deal with these verses in this manuscript. If God allows me a few more years, it will be dealt with in another book on the subject of marriage, a book that will show that divorce is never an option a believer needs to take. There is another more effective option with a lot fewer consequences and no guilt. Verses 1 through 9 of this chapter give us an example of the necessity of viewing Matthew in light of Jewish customs in order to arrive at Biblical conclusions about marriage and divorce. When viewed in the light of those customs, the passage sheds an understandable interpretation to what Jesus is actually teaching.

The rest of chapter 19, for our study, deals with two questions asked by the disciples. The first was in reference to the rich young ruler who came to Jesus to attempt to justify his lifestyle. Their question was in reference to the statement of our Lord when He commented, "...That a rich man shall hardly enter into the Kingdom of heaven. And again I say unto you, it is easier for a camel to go through the eye of a needle, than for a rich man to enter into the Kingdom of heaven." Their question was, "Who then can be saved?"

Thank God, that Jesus did not say that it was impossible for a rich man to be saved; only very difficult. Remember how many times Israel, upon being incredibly blessed by God, gradually turned away from God, trusting only in themselves and on occasion, other gods? When God blesses us we tend to go away from Him, trusting in ourselves and not in our Creator. This makes salvation impossible, "...for there is no other name under heaven whereby we must be saved:" the name of Jesus (Acts 4:12). Don't ever give up on the wealthy when sharing Christ with them. God loves them too. Remember, "...with God, all things are possible."

The second question reveals that as yet they had not gotten a hold of the nine attitudes with which Jesus began His class in chapter five. Let me paraphrase the question: "Lord, we have left everything behind to follow You. What is in it for us?"

Jesus answers gently, but truthfully in verses 28 through 30 and on into chapter twenty. He tells them that all who are born again (regeneration KJV) will be rewarded and that they will sit on twelve thrones judging the twelve tribes of Israel. But then He says, "The first shall be last and the last shall be first." After the Holy Spirit fell on the disciples in Acts 2, this question would never again cross the minds of these men, but the nine attitudes have not yet become a consistent part of their lives.

In chapter 20 of Matthew Jesus gives the parable about the farmer who hires workers, some at the beginning of the day, others at nine-o-clock, others at twelve noon, and still others at five-o-clock. All received the same wage. Those who worked all day complained. "They worked only an hour and we worked all day. Shouldn't we get more?" The farmer reminded them that they had contracted for a penny which represented a day's wage. That's what they received. It is his prerogative to give the others whatever he felt was right.

The message in this parable is that it is the new birth that determines our salvation, not our works. It is not about what we have done for Christ, but about what Christ has done for us and our acceptance of His grace by faith. It is not about how long we have been saved, but that we are saved. It is not about when we went into the field, but that we went into the field. Still, we are not to put off placing our trust in Christ. Upon our decision to trust in Jesus rests our entire eternity, heaven or hell, an eternity with God or an eternity separated from Him.

A man in East Springfield, Pennsylvania and a good friend of my father's, would chuckle each time Dad would talk to him about Christ and would say to Dad, "Some day, Augustine, you are going to get a call about two in the morning asking you to come to the hospital because I am dying. I want you to come as fast as you can and lead me to Christ." Dad told him that he would be glad to do that, but what if he did not have that chance? The sad end of the story is that Dad did get that call and it was about two in the morning. He did rush as fast as he could to Erie to the hospital, but when he arrived; his friend had lapsed into a coma and never regained consciousness. That is why Scripture tells us that, "...Now is the accepted time. Behold now is the day of salvation" (II Corinthians 6:2). That is why our calling to make disciples is so very urgent. Eternity hangs in the balance for all people. Our message is vital. There is no other way.

In verses 20 to 28 of Matthew twenty Jesus again focuses on the nine attitudes. His focus is triggered by the mother of Zebedee's children when she requests that her sons be allowed to sit next to Jesus in His Kingdom. The rest of the disciples became disenchanted with the two in question, but Jesus uses the occasion to underscore the importance of right attitudes.

In essence He said, "Unlike the world, if you want to be great in God's sight, you must serve each other. And the one who is the leader must have the heart of a servant. I am God and yet I did not come to be served, I came to serve and to lay down my life so you could live." Again and again, we see the awesome importance of these nine attitudes in becoming an effective force in reaching a lost world for the Savior.

Remember, there is nothing more important that you will ever do than the importance of introducing men and women to the Lord Jesus Christ, absolutely nothing!

CHAPTER FOURTEEN

JESUS LOVED HIS ENEMIES, DO YOU?

We now move to Matthew 23 in our training for discipleship. This does not infer that the chapters we skipped are not helpful in our training, but we are looking at those teachings of Jesus directed directly at the disciples and that begins again in chapter 23.

The key verse in our training manual is Matthew 5:20. Jesus is speaking: "For I say unto you, that except your righteousness shall exceed the righteousness of the scribes and Pharisees, ye shall in no case enter into the Kingdom of Heaven!" This message is profoundly felt in the words of Jesus in chapter 23. It is noted that Jesus is speaking to the multitude and to the disciples when He begins to warn them of the scribes and Pharisees (verse I). He tells then to respect the position, but not to follow their example. He calls them hypocrites, blind guides, lazy, arrogant, proud, bad examples, fools, blind, whited sepulchers full of bones, unclean, full of iniquity, children of prophet killers, serpents, a generation of vipers, killers and persecutors. He is not at all complementary to these failed religious leaders of His day.

A major part of the preparation of a disciple is that he avoid at all cost, the attitudes of the scribes and Pharisees and that is why Jesus began with the nine attitudes in chapter five. The flesh is self centered: the Spirit is Christ centered. The scribes and Pharisees cared only about themselves and wanted people to honor and respect them, but the true believer cares about the things of God and what he can do to please Christ. The true believer's attitudes include genuine humility, a hatred of sin accompanied by a love for sinners, more concern for the rights of others than his own, a desire to be like Christ, wanting to impress the Creator instead of people, a compassion for others when they fail and a desire to help restore them to fellowship with Christ. His motive is to please God in everything he does, a desire to introduce the lost to Jesus, a determination to obey God no matter what the cost and a resolve to accomplish God's plan regardless of the opposition.

None of the nine attitudes of chapter five were a part of the lives of the scribes and Pharisees Attitudes make all the difference in the world. When people see these nine attitudes as a vital part of your life, they will see 'Christ in you, the hope of glory.' Read Matthew 23 and notice what Jesus says about these religious leaders and then purpose never to be like them. It will probably be a struggle, for we all possess a sin nature, even after we have come to the Savior. The difference is that now we have the power to overcome temptation, to fight selfishness and to focus on God rather than self. (I Corinthian 10:13).

If you desire to be exalted, the only way is to humble yourself (Matthew 23:12). When you truly humble yourself, He will lift you up. If you lift yourself up, you will be knocked down. A true disciple does not resemble the scribes and Pharisees at all!

Read the rebuke Jesus lays on the scribes and Pharisees in this chapter and then look at verses 37 through 39 of the chapter. In spite of all that He said about these men, His love for them shows through as He laments over Jerusalem: "O Jerusalem, Jerusalem, you who kill prophets and stone them which are sent unto you, how often would I have gathered your children together even as a hen gathers her chickens under her wing, and you would not! Now you have nothing!" Can you sense the hatred Jesus has for the sin of the scribes and Pharisees? Their sin is destroying them. Jesus hates that sin. But He <u>loves</u> them. Pray that God will teach you how to do that. It begins with the right attitude.

This might be a good time to pause in your training for discipleship and meditate on the passage in Matthew 5: 43 through 48. Jesus admonishes us to love our enemies for He obviously loved His. Just feel His anger at the sin and stupidity of the scribes and Pharisees: it goes deep within His soul. Have you ever heard a more intense rebuke in any situation? He pounds and pounds them into the ground: He is relentless in His verbal attack, but still He loves them. While some of these men are tares, sown among the wheat, still others are just misguided leaders, eligible for eternal life. Remember Nicodemus in John, chapter three. He was a Pharisee that found Jesus and trusted in Him. Real love often hurts the one who loves and we sense that hurt in Jesus as He laments over these wicked leaders in verses 37 through 39.

How about your enemies? Do you pray for them? Can you humble yourself enough to ask God to give you the grace to actually love them? As you focus on developing the nine attitudes of chapter five, you will discover that the ability to love people who hurt you will become more and more a part of your love for Jesus as you grow in Him.

I recall a story that my Father used to share in his messages about a blacksmith in a frontier village during the days of the Old West in America. He was a rough and tough self-sufficient man who believed he needed no one, especially not God in his life and he tended to mock any one who seemed to need that 'crutch'. A farmer and his wife had a burden on their hearts to see this lost blacksmith come to the Savior so they prayed for him regularly and from time to time, when using his services, would share Christ with him. His response while always polite, included making light fun of their dependence upon God and assured the farmer that he needed no such faith, but the farmer and his wife refused to stop praying.

One night, the burden for this man so overwhelmed them that they stayed up all night praying for this man and toward morning, the farmer said to his wife, "I'm going into town to talk to him. He hooked up the buckboard and rode into town arriving about six in the morning, finding the blacksmith already at work. He went into the shop and greeted him, calling him by name and then said, "My wife and I have been up all night praying for you," and then, to his utter consternation, broke down in tears and wept convulsively. He tried to speak and could not, so embarrassed, he turned and got back into the buckboard and headed home.

When he got there his wife said to him, "How did it go?" "Terrible," he replied. "I told him we had been praying for him all night and then I began to weep and couldn't talk. It was so embarrassing. I really blew it!"

As they sat at the kitchen table, where they had been praying most of the night before, there was a knock at the door and when they answered it, they found the blacksmith standing there, a little nervous, but obviously seeking. They invited him in and offered him some coffee.

The blacksmith looked at them and shared his heart. "Many times you have told me about my need for God, and I just blew you off again and again, but when you came in this morning and told me that you and your wife had been up all night praying for me and then you started to cry, I had no answer for that. Please tell me why you care so much about me?" And in the story Dad told, they shared with him God's plan for his life and God, working through them, brought the man that morning to a saving knowledge of Jesus Christ.

Jesus loved His enemies. Look at the cross. "Father, forgive them, for they know not what they do (Luke 23:34). There is power in loving your enemies. Ask God to help you. It is a part of 'hungering and thirsting after righteousness. With God's help and only with God's help, you can do it!

CHAPTER FIFTEEN

ONE TO TWO HOURS A WEEK
IS ALL IT TAKES

In chapter twenty-four of Matthew the disciples approach Jesus privately to ask Him about the last days and what signs would indicate that those days were approaching. This question has been on their minds for most of the time they have been with the Lord, because it was a question the entire Jewish nation had been asking for centuries. They were under Roman rule and longed for their freedom. Doubtless this was one of the initial motivations that kept the disciples with Jesus for the three years of His earthly ministry.

Statements from the the disciples such as, "Send them away so they can get food" and actions which included forbidding children to come to Jesus, demonstrate that they still have not as yet plugged into the nine attitudes Jesus spoke of in chapter five. Still Jesus patiently continues to work with them, knowing that His efforts will one day result in disciples that will impact the world that He came to save.

We, too, look forward to the coming of Christ as did the disciples: the sooner the better. But for us who are committed to being obedient to the will of God and to going into the entire world to win and disciple the lost, it is a win, win situation. If Jesus comes today we continue into our eternal life which began when we accepted Christ as Savior and if He does not return just now, we have another day, week, month or year to fulfill His command to reach the world for Him. We can accomplish this if we are willing to invest one to two hours each week in witnessing and in making disciples. And remember, every success is a euphoric experience as God works through us to accomplish His incredible plan.

I am not going to attempt to dissect this chapter because you can read it for yourself. I also believe that when we share the passion of God for the lost as mentioned in II Peter 3:9, for He, "...is not willing that any should perish, but that all should come to repentance," we, like God would desire more time to reach these people for Christ. Because God loves them so much and we have grown to love them, we pray for more time so that we can be the conduit through which the Holy Spirit can bring them to the Savior. II Peter 3:10 assures us that,"...The day of the Lord will come..." make no mistake, He IS coming. In the meantime we can work to accomplish His will. For us it is a win, win situation! Verse 14 of this chapter tells us how we can speed up the return of Christ. "And this Gospel of the Kingdom shall be preached in all the world for a witness unto all nations; and then shall the end come." We want Him to return, so we do what it takes to reach the world. Mathematically speaking, we can do it in thirty-three years or less, just by investing one to two hours a week witnessing and making disciples. You are probably thinking, "He repeats that a lot in this book!" The repetition is by design. The purpose of this manuscript is to help each of us realize what we could accomplish, just by being faithful and consistent.

Jesus' message toward the end of chapter twenty-four is: "Be ready, for I am coming at a time when I am least expected." The Bible does not teach the soon return of Christ: rather it teaches the 'imminent' return of the Savior. What is the difference? 'Soon' means in a few hours, or days or weeks or months or years. When we proclaim the 'Soon' return of the Lord, it causes people to question that He is coming back at all. Peter writes in chapter three of his second epistle. They cry, "Where is He and why hasn't He returned? For since the Fathers fell asleep all things continue as they were." It has been two thousand years. Obviously He is not coming soon! His coming is <u>imminent</u>!

'Imminent' means any second, at a moment, at the twinkling of an eye: it means it could happen now. Paul believed in the imminent return of Christ. His return was as imminent then as it is now. It is obviously closer now than it was when Paul lived, but it is still imminent! The imminent return of Jesus is what we should be talking about to the world.

Jesus' message to the disciples and to us is, "Be ready, live as though I am coming in the next second: don't get caught napping. Let My Father find you busy when I come back. You have a job to do that will count for all eternity; don't fail! I'm counting on you!"

Remember, if you are the only one who decides to put this plan into practice, you have the potential to impact the whole world in thirty-three years. And if in each group of four, only one goes on, it will happen! If all four continue, WOW! But be patient. It starts slowly, but over the years, it multiplies. I can hear Christ saying to you in eternity, "Well done good and faithful servant!"

And remember, if one million believers take up the challenge, we can accomplish the goal Christ set before us in ten to thirteen years. Just think of it! If ten people in a given church attempt to do this, and they are only ten percent effective, in ten years that church will have one thousand-twenty-four new believers who are soul winning disciple makers.

In chapter 25, Jesus continues His emphasis on readiness for the second coming. He relates two 'Kingdom is like' stories. The first is the parable of the ten virgins; five wise and five foolish. The wise had done what was necessary to do to prepare for the coming of the bridegroom, the foolish had not. Neither group was expecting the bridegrooms' arrival, for when he came, they were all asleep; the wise and the foolish. When all were awakened at the bridegroom's arrival, the foolish wanted the wise to share their oil, but that is not possible: no one gets into heaven because of someone else's faith. So the foolish missed out on the wedding.

Oil in Scripture, often represents the Holy Spirit. The wise had the Holy Spirit within, for they had put their trust in Christ. The foolish were bent on getting into the wedding without this oil. They wanted to do things their way.

Jesus' message in this parable is, "Be ready, for no one knows when I will return!" There is also, in this story, a picture of the Church in our world today and that picture is in the statement, "While the bridegroom tarried, they all slumbered and slept." Yes: the wise and the foolish were all asleep and I believe that the Church, for the past one hundred years has been, for the most part, asleep. Had the wise been awake in the parable, some of those fools might have been encouraged to get oil while there was still time.

All around us are people who are lost and headed for a Christless eternity. God has called us to offer to them the same free gift that He has given to us. If we fail, they are lost! Now it is not possible that we will win them all and the Bible clearly tells us that all will not be saved. But we can win a few, one at a time. By teaching them discipleship for six months to a year, they in turn can win and disciple a few who will do the same. In a few short years the whole world will have at least heard the message and many will have been won to the Savior and possess the assurance of eternal life that we enjoy. All of heaven will rejoice each time someone places his trust in Christ. Don't go to sleep! We have all eternity to rest, and besides, we can accomplish this task by investing only a few short hours each week in the task.

The second parable deals with gifts and abilities that God gives to us to use to accomplish His will. The Bible reminds us that, "every good gift is from above" (James 1:17). If you have any special ability, and you use that ability, remember it was bestowed upon you by God. This is true even if you do not profess to know God through Christ. I love the statement made often by Rush Limbaugh, when he says, "With talent on loan from God!" If you are a Rush supporter or not, you need to know that the statement is absolutely true. All of our skills, abilities, talents and even our aptitudes are 'on loan from God' and at death they will all be returned to Him.

In this parable Jesus is urging us to use what we have been given to accomplish His will for our lives, which includes reaching the world for Him. Remember, we are not saved by works (Ephesians 2:8 & 9), but we are saved to work (Ephesians 2:10). God wants us to worship together, to spend quality time with our families and friends, to work to provide for our families, to spend time getting away to rest and relax and enjoy the beautiful world He has loaned to us, but we can do all that and still use our talents and abilities to reach the lost for Him. One to two hours a week if used wisely will accomplish the assignment.

In the parable, burying our talent leads to incredibly undesirable consequences. My take on that is that those who bury their talent do not know the Lord and profess to know Him for all the wrong reasons. Those who know the Lord will want to please the Lord, not to be saved or to stay saved, but because they are saved. If this is not your desire, it would be a good time to follow Paul's admonition and, "Examine yourself, whether you are in the faith" (II Corinthians 13:5).

In verses 31 through the end of the chapter, Jesus provides His disciples with the blueprint for bringing the lost to Christ. He tells them that in His Kingdom, He will separate the sheep from the goats (the saved from the lost). The sheep He will place on His right hand and the goats on His left.

He speaks first to the sheep, inviting them to inherit the Kingdom prepared for them by God. This is yours, he tells them, because you followed the blueprint put forth by God. He told them that they had fed Him when He was hungry, given Him water when He was thirsty, welcomed Him when He was a stranger, clothed Him when He was naked, visited Him when He was sick and ministered to Him when He was in prison. The righteous are flabbergasted! Lord, we don't remember ever seeing You in any of these situations: how could this be? Jesus answered, "Inasmuch as ye did it to one of the least of these my brethren, ye have done it unto Me."

There is the blueprint. There is the channel for witness. We feed the hungry, we give water to the thirsty, we welcome strangers, we give clothes to the needy, and we minister to people who are sick and in prison: these are ways to make contact with lost people and show them the love of Christ through our actions and love for them.

The goats heard bad news. They had not done any of these things for the right reasons. They did not know the Lord, they had not placed their trust in Christ alone for their salvation, they did not possess the fruits of the Spirit as seen in Galatians 5:22, and therefore had not made the nine attitudes of Matthew, chapter 5 a part of their lives. They were self centered instead of Christ centered. So these people go away into everlasting punishment, but the righteous into life eternal.

I would like to bring this chapter to a close on this note. Some people teach that there will be no tears in heaven. If that is the case, how is Jesus going to wipe away every tear from our eyes? If there are no tears, there can be no wiping. Let me tell you what I think is going to happen.

Remember, this is only my speculation on the passage and I could be way off base, but this is what I think. In eternity, God is going to show us our lives and all the things we might have accomplished had we not been asleep and opportunities we missed because we were not in tune with His Spirit. As we view these missed opportunities, we are going to weep like we have never wept before, completely broken because of our failure to do all that He wanted us to do. Then He is going to erase it all from our memories to be remembered no more and that is how He will wipe away all tears from our eyes! (...The former shall not be remembered nor come into mind. Isaiah 65:17)

In all probability, none of us will have done as much as we should have done or as much as we could have done, but let's do all that we know how to do from this time forward to reach a lost world for Christ. Remember, one to two hours of additional time every week, used in the power of the Holy Spirit, will make it work Are you willing to make the commitment?

CHAPTER SIXTEEN

WHAT? COULD YOU NOT WATCH WITH ME ONE HOUR?
OR
CAN YOU NOT INVEST ONE TO TWO HOURS EVERY WEEK?

As we approach these last three chapters of Matthew's Gospel, it is obvious that a great deal of the disciple's training and learning came from the example of Jesus' everyday life. Peter tells us in his first epistle, chapter 2, verse 21 that Jesus, in His suffering, left, "…us an example that we should follow in His steps." These examples have been presented to us many times through preaching, Sunday School, Seminars, special classes and in our own personal Bible study so I will not go into very much detail in these chapters. I just want to make a few observations that I hope will be helpful in your quest for real discipleship.

The first deals with the precious expensive ointment pored out on the feet of Jesus at the house of Simon the Leper in verses 6 through 13 of Matthew twenty-six. The disciples complained about what they considered a waste of money. "This could have been sold and the money used for the poor," they cried! But Jesus corrects them.

A very important truth shouts to us from this story. Always remember that our number one focus is <u>Jesus</u>, not lost people. In Mark 1:35 through 38 Jesus rises early in the morning to spend time with His Father, even though there were people who desired to see Him. Time with the Father was far more important than ministry to the multitudes whom He loved.

The importance of the personal relationship we enjoy with our Lord far exceeds the necessity of winning the lost. In fact, it is our love for Christ that will drive us to invest those one to two hours each week in the lives of others, for that is what Christ has commanded us to do. Obedience is the highest form of worship. The greater our love for the Savior, the more zeal we will show for winning the lost to Him.

In verses 26 through 29 of Matthew twenty-six, Jesus has what we call communion with the twelve. His purpose was that they and that we remember what was about to happen.

Our Catholic Friends, when celebrating The Lord's Supper, teach that the bread and wine become the literal body and blood of Jesus. Jesus did say, "This is My body," and "This is My blood." While I disagree with their theology, I admire their reasoning. They are taking the words of Jesus literally.

Jesus instituted the Communion Service to remind us of the incredible sacrifice that He made for us on the Cross, without which no one could be saved or possess eternal life (Luke 22:19). The fact is that we as believers in Jesus are temples of the Holy Spirit (I Corinthians 3:16, 6:19 & 20): Christ dwells in each of us. Jesus told the people in John 6:53 & 54, "Except ye eat the flesh of the Son of Man, and drink His blood, ye have no life in you. Whoever eats My flesh and drinks My blood has eternal life; and I will raise him up at the last day; For My flesh is meat indeed and My blood is drink indeed. He that eats My flesh and drinks My blood dwells in Me and I in him."

When you accepted Christ as your personal Savior, a number of events took place in your life. One of them was that the Holy Spirit, the Spirit of God, came to dwell in you (Romans 8:9). To receive Christ by faith is to 'eat His flesh and drink His blood' because His Spirit now indwells you. When we take Communion, since His spirit is already within us, we have already eaten His flesh and have already quenched our spiritual thirst with His blood. This reminder is so incredibly significant and we should do it often (I Corinthians 11:26). In communion we are being reminded of Christ's great sacrifice and it is a vital part of our worship. Remember, effective worship makes us more effective soul winners (Proverbs 11:30).

Reading verses 36 through 46 of Matthew twenty-six we are reminded of the need to stay awake. While Jesus agonized in the Garden of Gethsemane He needed the support of His disciples. Had they not fallen asleep, would the burden of Christ that weekend been somewhat lightened? I do not know, but I do know that Jesus was disappointed in them because at such a crucial point in His life on earth, they could not stay awake. Had they understood what was about to happen, it might have made a difference. Without the death and resurrection of Jesus, the world would have no hope at all. The event that is about to take place has to be viewed as the most important event in the history of mankind: nothing else even comes close. The disciples did not understand.

As you consider the millions still outside of Christ and their fate should they fail to receive Him, every opportunity that permits you to be used of God in bringing one more individual to the Savior has to be the second most important event in your life and in the life of the one with whom you are investing your time. Jesus words to His disciples are haunting words: "What! Could you not watch with Me one hour?" Might He be saying to us: "Could you not invest just one to two hours a week in someone to help them become one of My disciples?" I am not adding to the words of Jesus, but this is what I hear Him saying in Matthew 28, verses 18 through 20.

The trial and crucifixion Jesus suffered is an example to us that we should follow in His steps (I Peter 2:21). During this horrendous experience, He was humble, He hated sin enough to give His own life to cleanse us from it, He surrendered all His rights, He was the righteousness of God, He showed mercy (Father, forgive them), His motive was love, His death brought salvation to all who believe, and He handled persecution and false accusations with confidence and assurance. Is it any wonder that the witness of the Roman Centurion was, "…Truly this was the Son of God!"

Do you see how important our attitude is in making our witness effective? This might be a good time to go back and read chapters 3, 4 and 5 of this book again and ask God to help you make these principles a part of your personality. The more you allow these attitudes to become a part of the real you, the more God can use you to encourage people with whom you share Christ to be encouraged to respond positively to the message.

Please forgive me! I know many of you as you read this book, have many of these characteristics in your life already, but I know that I am still working on them and that there is always room for improvement. In fact, when we are convinced we have all of them down pat, we need to go back and work on the first one a little more. Paul said, "I die daily" (I Corinthians 15:31), and so should we! Much as an athlete, no matter how good, never totally masters the fundamentals of the game, so we will never totally master the nine fundamentals needed to effectively live for Christ. There is always room for improvement.

Following the resurrection, Jesus remained on earth just long enough to establish confirmation of His rising from the dead and then His work on earth was done. He could return to Heaven. His work is completed, but ours is not. What an honor that He turned the work over to His disciples and to us to complete the task of building His Church. His parting words to them and to us were these: "...All power is given unto Me in heaven and in earth. Go ye, therefore, and teach all nations, baptizing them in the name of the Father, and of the son, and of the Holy Spirit, Teaching them to observe all things whatsoever I have commanded you, lo, I am with you always, even unto the end of the world."

CHAPTER SEVENTEEN

By James P. Augustine

A NECESSARY PERSPECTIVE IN SUCCESSFUL SOUL WINNING

"I am the vine; you are the branches. If a man remains in me and I in him, he will bear much fruit; apart from me you can do nothing." John 15:5

When I was young, my family and I would drive to Montana often to see my Grandmother. It was a long trip, consisting of three days of travel. During our trip, my father would often stop and pick up fruit for us to eat. We didn't know it then, but the reason for this pickup was to keep us from having to stop for lunch on the road, or breakfast in the morning. But it was on those trips that I developed an appreciation for fruit.

But it wasn't until I was married that I developed an appreciation for vegetables. In fact, I was horrified of my veggies, and would often refuse to eat them. But my wife very calmly and kindly helped me to start appreciating my vegetables.

In the course of time, however, I have developed an appreciation for most things that grow. In fact, fruit is the subject of one of the first things that a person will draw, paint or sculpt in art class. Why? It is because fruit is colorful, shapely, and has a use that goes far beyond the sum of its parts.

But what would happen if the branches of the trees and the vines and the bushes that bear the fruit and vegetables became tired of just hanging around and dealing with the fruit. I don't get any respect. I don't need any tree or bush or vine to tell me what I can and can't bear." What would happen? Aside from someone sending you to the loony-bin for listening to branches, we'd have no more fruit!

Man Overboard!

The story is told of a man who was crossing the Atlantic by ship. A little while into the voyage, a violent storm arose on the sea. And as he felt the tossing and turning of the boat in the water he ran down to his cabin with an incredible seasickness.

As he lay there trying to get his stomach to get back in line, he heard the call of "MAN OVERBOARD!" His initial thought was to go and see what he could do to help, but realizing his predicament, he stayed where he was.

Not too long after, he had a prodding in his spirit to put his lantern in the portal of his cabin. So he got up and put his lantern in the portal and laid back down to get over his sickness.

Once the storm had subsided and he got his sea legs back underneath him, he went back to the top deck where the men were standing around and discussing the events of the previous night.

"It was unbelievable," said one man. "I was going down for the last time and thought that all hope was lost. I was going under and darkness surrounded me. When all of a sudden a light from a portal on the ship shone down directly on my hand as I was going under and a man grabbed my hand and pulled me up to safety! That one light saved my life."

We may not understand the things that God asks us to do. We may not even like the things He asks us to do. But when we are obedient, we see God work in ways we never imagined.

Important Truth

In John chapter 15, Jesus reveals something about Himself that helps us understand this whole idea of discipleship. In fact, I believe it is the very key to being an effective disciple of Christ.

Chapter 15 of the book of John is a most interesting chapter. It falls within the discourse between Jesus and His disciples in the upper room during the evening meal of Passover (or what we in the Christian community have dubbed, "The Last Supper").

So if we go back to the beginning of this discourse (chapter 13), we see Jesus starting to tell His disciples some of the things that they will need if they are to reach the world for Him.

He begins by showing them (and us) the importance of humility and being willing to do those things that seem unimportant or beneath us.

He then reveals His betrayer to John, tells them that He is going to die and rise again, gives them the command to love one another, and tells Peter that he's going to deny Him three times.

In chapter 14, He encourages them to trust God and to trust Him because He is going to the Father. He tells them that He is the Way, the Truth and the Life, and that no one comes to the Father but through Him. He tells them that those who remain in Him will be close to the Father and that they will do even greater things. He lets them know that He is going to send the Holy Spirit. He tells them that those who love Him will obey Him (this is key to what we're talking about as well), and that He is going away, but will come back.

And that brings us to Jesus' discourse on the vine. It was one of the things that Jesus found to be so important that we have to grab hold of this if we want to be the effective disciples of Christ that we need to be to see this task accomplished.

The Vine
Jesus tells His disciples that He is the Vine. He is saying that He is the source...the channel through which the power of God moves to give life to the branches. He also tells His disciples that they are the branches...they are the ones

through whom the power of God (from the vine) moves to reveal Jesus to the world.

There is something that I learned not too long ago that revolutionized how I looked at these verses of Scripture. Did you know that the branch of a vine (or a tree or a bush for that matter) doesn't produce anything on its own? Now I am sure that many of you who are gardeners or farmers realized that, but to one who doesn't have a green thumb (like me) it was a new concept.

To illustrate this, think about when a branch falls off of one of the trees in your yard. Does the branch continue living? Or does it die? The trunk of the tree continues to live, but unless the branch stays connected to the source of life (the trunk) it cannot bear any fruit.

Remain

So Jesus tells us that we must remain in Him if we can ever hope to bear fruit. What does this mean for us as we go about the task of making disciples? It means that it is not about us! It's about Him! He tells us at the end of verse five very plainly, "without me you can do nothing."

Notice this word, "nothing." In the original Greek, it is the strongest word to indicate nothing. It really means that it is a zero (which is nothing) with the circle removed (which is less than nothing). We cannot do a single thing if it were not for Jesus (the vine) at work in us and through us.

I laugh in my spirit when I hear people say things like, "Pastor, this is what I am doing for God!" I laugh inside because I think, "Oh really? You mean to tell me that God couldn't get that done without you?" You see, I understand what people are saying, and I understand that we need to do things for God's glory, but we *have* to understand that there is NOTHING we can do for God. Anything that we accomplish for the Kingdom is because of the power of God at work in our lives. When we remain in Christ, we are then able to tap into the power of God that will allow us to do the things that God has prepared for us to do.

God's Workmanship

An important point to remember here is from Ephesians 2:10, where we are told that we are God's masterpiece, created to do the works that were prepared for us since the beginning of the world.

You see, you and I were not saved simply to go to heaven. If that were the case, the moment we received Christ as our Savior, we would go to heaven, because that's our purpose. No, we were saved to do good works.

The works that are accomplished through us are what Jesus calls "fruit" in John 15. And when we look at the fact that we are simply the branches on the vine, we realize that we don't produce the fruit. We are simply the conduit through which the nutrients can flow and the fruit is born on the end of the branch.

Friend, there is nothing that you do *for* Jesus. It is all Him, and it will always be Him doing the work through you. Our job is to simply remain in the vine and allow Him to work through us. Then the fruit that God wants us to bear will be evident to the world around us.

The Proof

In verse 9 of chapter 15, Jesus gives us a glimpse into the evidence of a life that is connected to vine. He says, "As the Father has loved me, so have I loved you. Now remain in my love. If you obey my commands, you will remain in my love, just as I have obeyed my Father's commands and remain in his love. I have told you this so that my joy may be in you and that your joy may be complete. My command is this: Love each other as I have loved you. Greater love has no one than this that he lay down his life for his friends." Jesus is saying that we remain in His love by obeying His commandments. Friends, how obedient are we to what God has called us to do? How much do we love God? He told us that we are to love Him with all our hearts, all our souls, all our minds, and all our strength. Do we truly love God that much?

He also told us that we are to love our neighbor as ourselves. Do we truly love those around us as much as we love ourselves? If we don't, we are not remaining in the vine! And if we are not in the vine, we can not hope to accomplish the tasks that God has for us to do.

The proof (or fruit) of our lives must be love...love for our brothers and sisters in Christ, and for those yet to receive Him. We are called to this, my brothers and sisters: we must love one another, showing ourselves to be Christ's disciples.

The Bottom Line

Francis Xavier, who lived in the 16th century, once wrote:

> "My God, I love Thee; not because
> I hope for heaven thereby,
> Nor yet because who love Thee not
> Are lost eternally.
>
> Thou, O my Jesus, Thou didst me
> Upon the cross embrace;
> For me didst bear the nails, and spear,
> And manifold disgrace,
>
> And griefs and torments numberless,
> And sweat of agony;
> Yea, death itself; and all for me
> Who was thine enemy.
>
> Then why, O blessed Jesus Christ,
> Should I not love Thee well?
> Not for the sake of winning heaven,
> Nor of escaping hell;

Not from the hope of gaining aught,
Not seeking a reward;
But as Thyself hast loved me,
O ever-loving Lord.

So would I love Thee, dearest Lord,
And in Thy praise will sing;
Solely because Thou art my God,
And my most loving King.

Francis Xavier knew that love for God, love for Jesus meant that something had to give. He knew that loving Jesus is what we do, not just because of what He's done for us, but because we are bearing the fruit that HE ALONE can produce.

My friend, I want to give you a challenge. The challenge is not to love God more. It is not to seek to be a better person or a better Christian. It's not to allow yourself to be all that you can be for Christ. These are good goals and we should strive for them, but that is not the challenge that I want to put before you today. The challenge that I want you to focus on is this:

WILL YOU ALLOW THE VINE TO WORK THROUGH YOU?

As we've already stated, our love for Jesus is demonstrated in our obedience to Him. And if you and I are going to truly love Jesus, we must first allow Him to work through us. You are a branch that is (I hope) in the vine. And if you are in the

Vine, then you have to ask yourself the question, "Do I see the fruit of Love being born out in my life?"

So I want you today, if you are willing to allow God to work through you, to take a pen and piece of paper and proclaim to yourself and to God that you are NO LONGER going to just be a spectator, a consumer, but one who will be doing what God's Word tells you to do. If that is where you are today, lay aside this book for a moment and write a note to God that says that you will follow Him and do your best (with His help) to demonstrate the Love of God to the world around you.

CHAPTER EIGHTEEN

"MOVING SLOWLY IN THE RIGHT DIRECTION IS THE FASTEST WAY TO GET THERE"

We have now completed our basic training for discipleship from the book of Matthew. There are other things to learn along the way, but what we have learned already will get us off to a good start. In this chapter we want to think about the 'how to' of discipleship or in other words, where do we go from here?

Step one: Lay aside the one to two hours that you are dedicating specifically to this assignment each week. This time will be used to:

1. Pray for the person you will introduce to Christ

2. Pray for God's leading in finding that person

3. Go places for the specific purpose of meeting people who need the Lord.

4. Visit people with needs for the purpose of letting Christ meet that need through you and provide an opportunity to share your faith

5. Disciple one on one using the five steps material

6. Work with your small group of four until they are ready to reach new people for Christ.

<u>Step two</u>: When you find the person with whom you are going to share your faith, pray for wisdom, direction and for God's timing. Be ready for that moment when you can present God's plan of salvation to them. The plan is simple enough for a child to understand and complex enough to baffle people with college degrees. God's timing is vital.

<u>WHAT IS NECESSARY IN BECOMING A CHRISTIAN</u>?

<u>First</u>: To become a Christian, to possess eternal life, one must first <u>recognize his/her need for a Savior</u>. We must realize that we are sinners and that we cannot deal with our sin problem alone.

<u>Second</u>: We need to understand that we are <u>fully responsible for our sinful condition and repent</u>. We need to experience genuine remorse for our sin. The Bible tells us that we are sinners by birth (Psalm 51:5), we are sinners by choice (Romans 7:15-20), and we are sinners by divine decree (Romans 3:23).

<u>Third</u>: We need to understand that the <u>price of our sin is death</u> (eternal separation from God Romans 6:33a)

Fourth: We need to realize that <u>Jesus' death on the cross was payment in full</u> for our sin (Romans 5:8).

<u>Fifth</u>: We need to <u>trust in Jesus Christ by faith</u>. This includes believing that His death was full payment for our sin. His purpose in coming to this world was not to condemn us in our sin, but to save us from our sin (Ephesians 2:8 & 9, John 3:17). John 1:12 tells us that, "To as many as received Him, to them he gave power to become children of God, to them that believe on His name."

One of the results of trusting Jesus is everlasting life! It is not because we are worthy: it is not because we earned it: it is not because we have merited it: it is because He loves us and paid the debt in full (John 3:16)!

There are a number of tools available that you can use when leading an individual to the Lord. "Campus Crusade for Christ" has some excellent material. "The Navigators" have put out very helpful booklets and there are other reputable organizations that have published material you may find helpful.

I have used a little booklet produced by a company called "Evantell" in Dallas, Texas (www.evantell.org). The booklet is called, "May I Ask You a Question?" It uses four verses and four illustrations to present the plan of salvation. It is simple and easily understood. I like this little booklet, not only for its easily understood format, but for the lead question that is an automatic conversation opener. You are in conversation with someone about any subject and then you ask them, "May I Ask You a Question?"

The response is almost always, "Sure!"

Then you ask, "Has anyone ever taken a Bible and shown you how you can know for certain that you have eternal life, that you will never die and that you will go to heaven? Has anyone ever done that for you?

"No!"

"May I?"

If they answer, "Yes," then you share the material in the booklet. If the answer is in the negative, my counsel is to simply say, "O, Jesus Christ has made such a dramatic impact in my life and the lives of my family that I thought you might be interested in hearing about it, but that's okay: Let's talk about something else: How about those Rays?"

Sometimes, the fact that you are not pressuring them will create an opening that will allow you to share Christ with them, or increase the possibility that, later on, someone else will be able to share with them. One plants, one waters, but God gives the increase. I am aware that Paul wrote in II Corinthians 5:11: "Knowing therefore the terror of the Lord, we persuade men." That explains part of our motivation for witnessing, but I am not convinced that an individual who accepts the Lord simply because I put forth a good argument, is really saved. Sometimes it can be effective so let the Holy Spirit guide you in your approach.

When sharing the plan of salvation with people, I often encourage them not to embrace Christ as a favor to me. I assure them that I will love them even if they choose not to accept Christ. If they pray the sinner's prayer to please me, they have accomplished nothing. This prayer will only be meaningful if the individual has come to the realization that he/she needs a Savior, it's not about pleasing any other person. God has children: He has no grandchildren.

If you have questions about how to bring someone to Christ, ask your pastor for help. Just as someone introduced you to Christ, so you must be ready to introduce others to Him (I Peter 3:15).

<u>Step three</u>: Once this new believer has prayed the sinner's prayer with you, you need to invite him/her to spend one hour a week with you for the next five weeks. These will be their first five steps toward discipleship.

For sessions one through four, I use material put out by Multiplication Ministries in Vista, California (Post Office Box 1270, Zip Code 92085-1270)

The pamphlets are titled as follows:
Session 1. Assurance of Salvation
Session 2. The Quiet Time
Session 3. Christ Centered Fellowship
Session 4. Action Steps to an Abundant Life

For session five I use the booklet put out by Evantell called, "May I Ask You a Question?"

<u>Session 1 is about assurance</u>. What is unique about the pamphlet I use is that the new believer looks up verses in the Bible to answer the questions in the pamphlet, and all the verses in this first pamphlet are found in the gospel of John. If they can count, they can find the verses, thus giving them a sense of confidence that the Bible is a book that they can understand. It's not that difficult!

<u>Session 2 is about reading and understanding the Word of God</u>. It is very elementary, but remember, they may be perusing the Book for the very first time in his life.

<u>Session 3 deals with the importance of Christian fellowship in a local church</u>. While they will be spending six months to a year with you, it is important that they become independent of you so that they can eventually disciple others as meeting and growing with other believers is essential.

<u>Session 4 is a discussion of how to live for Christ in the power of the Holy Spirit</u>, not one's own power. No one is able to live for Christ without the grace God freely gives to us. We need to constantly depend on His power to keep us and to give us the strength necessary to live victoriously.

Session 5 is the session where <u>you demonstrate to them how to lead someone else to Christ</u>. This tends to be missing from most discipleship training programs. You use the booklet, "May I Ask You a Question," and show them how to use it when dealing with others. The ability to communicate your faith with others is absolutely necessary in the life of every disciple. Until you can share your faith with someone else, you are not a full fledged disciple. Other skills and attitudes are necessary to be an effective disciple, but this ability is essential.

If you choose to use the above mentioned material, plan to practice sharing it with another Christian until you become fully familiar with it. As the person discovers the answers to the questions in the Bible verse, respond with excitement and enthusiasm, encouraging them in their ability to understand. Don't zero in on just one right answer. In some cases there may be several responses that are correct from the passage. Never say, "You are wrong!" If the answer given is totally wrong, find a gentle way to point out the important truth so that he learns, but does not become afraid to answer the next question. On the advice of Jesus, "Be as wise as serpents and as harmless as doves."

Then practice presenting the gospel, using the "May I Ask You a Question?" booklet with another believer until it is a part of your entire thought process. If you feel more comfortable with other material, become as familiar as possible with it, asking other Christians to help you in your preparation. In other words, practice on them.

Now you are ready for step four! Once you have completed the five one on one sessions, invite this new convert to join you and two other people in forming a small group that will meet once a week or once every two weeks for about an hour, over a period of six months to a year for the purpose of encouraging each other in becoming effective, vibrant disciples of Jesus. Your task now is to find two other Christians and tell them that you need their help to disciple this new Christian and would they be willing to make such a commitment? You will be training three to be disciples. Look for vibrant believers who would like to be soul winners, but as yet are doing very little about it.

The length of time you spend with the group (six months to a year) will depend on the members of the group. Ask God for wisdom to discern when the group is ready to launch out on their own. Continue to keep in touch so that you can encourage each other as you begin new groups.

If you continue to work one on one after the five steps, it can be effective, but if, at the end of the year, your protégé decides not to continue, the chain is broken and that can be discouraging. Working with three plus yourself as a group, encouraging each other to go on after the year is over, increases the chances of at least one of the three going on and with the three of you encouraging each other, the probability of all three continuing is pretty good.

What material would the four of you study in your group over the six month to a year period? The answer to that question is, "The Word of God," the Bible! The first seventeen chapters of this book will help you as you study it in relation to a study of the book of Matthew, which is basic discipleship training.

Look at Matthew as if you are being trained by Christ, Himself. Spend a lot of time discussing the nine attitudes of Matthew in chapter 5 with the desire to make these attitudes a part of your overall personality. Discuss ways to avoid being like the scribes and Pharisees. Jesus mentions this over and over again in His training: It was a major concern of our Lord. I believe that the nine attitudes of Matthew 5 are crucial to reaching our greatest effectiveness as soul winners and disciplers.

Practical experiences can be planned as well. Just as Jesus sent the twelve out to practice, so you can plan trips to a mall, or a fair, or some other place where you can befriend people and share with them. Some will rebuff you in your attempt to share with them, but that is good experience for you. Come back to the group later and share experiences, talking about how you can be even more effective in communicating the Good News of the Gospel.

There is other material out there as well. Use material that you understand and that you are comfortable with, but be sure the material you use is <u>Bible centered</u> and <u>Bible based</u>.

REMEMBER

When you lead someone to Christ, you have <u>added</u> to the church. Praise God! Heaven is rejoicing!

When you teach the person you introduced to Christ to lead someone else to Christ, you are <u>adding</u> to the Church!
Heaven, again, rejoices!

BUT

When you teach the person you introduced to Christ to teach the one they brought to the Savior to lead someone else to Christ and to disciple him, NOW you are <u>multiplying</u>!

It is important to remember that the Bible is clear: we are not going to win everybody. Still Jesus admonishes us to preach the Gospel to every creature (Mark 16:15). Many will say, "No!" Even then, you have accomplished Christ's purpose in presenting the Gospel to every creature. If we do not give up, everyone will eventually hear the good news.

You can win thousands for Christ and not even scratch the surface as far as the world is concerned, or you can invest your life in one for six months to a year, spending one to two hours every week, and shake the whole world! If you are an effective adder, don't stop adding. Just chose one or two that come to Christ each year to disciple and together we can impact the whole world for the Savior.

If you are the one that is determined to become a real disciple and make this work, I will be praying for you. If not, you are going to miss an incredible blessing (EUPHORIA), but I would add: don't do this as a favor to me! I will like you regardless of what you do. If you choose to do this, do it because you are convinced that it is what God wants you to do. Do it for Him and give Him all praise and glory. Remember we can only bear fruit if we abide in the vine. Only Jesus can produce fruit. We are called of God to bear it. May you bear much fruit!

MOVING SLOWLY IN THE RIGHT DIRECTION IS THE FASTEST WAY TO GET THERE!

Remember the words of Jesus in Matthew 4:19, as He called His Disciples, His instructions were:

"FOLLOW ME AND I WILL MAKE YOU FISHERS OF MEN!"
True Disciples are soul winners!
Happy hunting and fishing!

CHAPTER NINETEEN

"A SPECIAL ADMONITION FOR PASTORS"

As you contemplate the words you have just finished reading, I want to encourage you in your effort to fulfill the great commission. In order to do this, I must remind you that God has not called us to build our church, or even a church! He has called us to build His Church! A promise that He made to us in Matthew 6:33 was this: "Seek first the kingdom of God and His righteousness, and everything else will fall into place." (Augustine's paraphrase)

When building a local church, we are often satisfied at least in part, with someone who fills the pew on Sunday and does little else. When you build His church, the result, more times than not, is a member of your church who is producing other disciples, who in turn reach others for Christ. It requires focus, and time invested, but the results are eternal!

I would encourage you to pick a small group of people, perhaps your Elder Board, Deacon Board or a select group of your flock who has a heart for God and systematically train them to do what is suggested in chapter eighteen. The number you work with is not as important as the quality of time you spend with them. Jesus worked with twelve very effectively. As you build men and women into soul winning disciplers, you will be guaranteeing the continued growth of your church; long after your ministry there is complete.

A lot of people in a building do not necessarily reflect the growth of Christ's Church even though others tend to be impressed with the presence of sheer numbers.

Will this approach take time? You bet it will. But remember:

MOVING SLOWLY IN THE RIGHT DIRECTION IS THE FASTEST WAY TO GET THERE!

Ten years from now your church will be full and you may even be planting new churches. May our Lord continue to bless you as you work to fulfill your calling to build Christ's Church.

EPILOGUE

WHERE THERE IS NO VISION,
THE PEOPLE PERISH

What I have attempted to do in the pages of this book is to convey a vision of a plan that could actually reach the world for Christ in thirty-three years or less. Will it happen? I don't know, but there is no doubt in my mind that it could happen even if only a few choose to follow the plan. Is this the only plan that will work? Probably not! If there is a better, more effective plan or vision, we need to plug it in.

If you dedicated yourself to invest an average of two hours a week to soul winning and discipleship training via the small group of four (including yourself) the worst that could happen is that over your lifetime one person a year would embrace the Savior and one to four would begin the next year with a vision to reach one more. In all probability you would accomplish more than you are accomplishing now.

Don't misunderstand. What you are already doing is probably incredibly significant in impacting the world for Christ, so keep on doing those things. Just add a few more minutes each week to focus on reaching one lost person and helping him/her to become a soul winner.

What excites me about this approach is that it is based on the training of the Master Himself and look at what His disciples accomplished, once they caught the vision.

From a purely mathematical perspective, this will work! Pray for guidance. You can make a difference!

One more challenge. Would you be willing to give to Jesus Christ all that there is of you: to lay your life completely at His feet?

Years ago, Mary and I were given the challenge of directing a teen choir in East Springfield. One of the songs the choir sang was a piece by Ken Medema called, "Moses." The text of the song is the confrontation of God and Moses at the burning bush. God asks Moses, "What is that in your hand, Moses?" "A rod," is the reply. God tells Moses to throw it down on the ground. Now the rod was the instrument used by Moses to make his living: he was a shepherd. But in obedience to God, he throws it down and it becomes a serpent. Then God commands him to pick up the snake and it becomes a rod again.

In the song God asks Moses, "Do you know what it means, Moses? Do you know what I am trying to say?

The rod of Moses became the rod of God (Exodus 4:20)!

With the rod of God, strike the rock and the water will come. With the rod of God, part the waters of the sea. With the rod of God, you can strike 'old' Pharaoh dead. With the rod of God you can set the prisoner free!

When you give God what is yours, He makes it His own and then gives most of it back to you to use to accomplish His will. As the song comes to a close, it asks the question, "What do you have in your hand today? To what, or to whom are you bound? Are you willing to give it to God right now?" Then the admonition, "Give it up! Let it go! Throw it down!" In other words lay it at the feet of the Master and watch Him use you to change lives. You become a channel through which Christ can reach the world. Think about it!

IF YOU HAVE NO VISION, THE LOST WILL PERISH. MAY GOD BLESS YOU AS YOU PRAY FOR HIS LEADING!

ACKNOWLEDGEMENTS

To list everyone that God has used in my life to bring about this text would be an impossible task. In some cases I remember the source, but in most I do not. Solomon wrote in Ecclesiastes that "There is nothing new under the sun." Without a doubt there is nothing new in this book. We have had the Book of Matthew for hundreds of years. I have simply taken that which God has taught me over the years through many of His faithful servants and with their help, attempted to project a vision that would enable believers to win the world for Christ in one generation. If you use one person's idea it is called plagiarism, but if you use the ideas of many it is called research.

Creativity is the result of a poor memory. I do not profess to be creative.

One of the people under whom I have studied is my father, Rev. Dr. P. H. Augustine. It was his tutelage that brought me the most of my pastoral training. What an awesome privilege! He possessed the nine attitudes of Matthew five and lived them as I have seen in very few other human beings. I will always be grateful for what I learned from him (I should have learned even more, but you know kids!).

There are many others God has used in my life. I was intending to list some of them, but as I started, I realized that it would be an impossible task. Just know this: that what I learned from many of you, I have attempted to commit to faithful men/women through my preaching and my counseling and through the writing of this book, with the hope that you will share what you learn with other faithful people who will, in turn share the same with others also. All that we accomplish together will be to His glory, who died for us and rose again that we might have life, and have it more abundantly.

ABOUT THE AUTHORS

WAYNE AUGUSTINE

Wayne C. Augustine was born on September 1, 1939 to Rev. Dr. and Mrs. P. H. Augustine. Even though raised in a pastor's home, it was not until he was thirteen years of age that he gave his life to Christ. After graduating from high school in 1957, he attended Taylor University in Upland Indiana. Prior to graduation he took a year off from his studies to travel with Jack Wyrtzen as a part of the Word of Life Quartet and then returned to Taylor to finish his degree in education with a major in math and physics, and a minor in Physical Education.

After graduation he became teacher, Athletic Director and coach at Berkshire Christian College in Lenox Massachusetts, where after two building years his basketball teams compiled a record of 54 wins and 21 losses, finishing his final season at 25 and 2. It was during this time that God continued to demonstrate that the seemingly impossible was never impossible if God was in it.

After five years of working with the wonderful people (teachers, students and friends) of the college, God led Wayne and Mary, his wife, to East Springfield to work with his father in the Federated Church. For twenty-six years he and Mary served the church, first as Camp Director (WLD Ranch), then as youth pastor and Christian Education Director, then associate Pastor and finally as senior pastor for sixteen years. During these years he and Mary founded and conducted, "Family Foundations Seminars" which provided opportunities to encourage and assist other pastors and their churches in the area of family counseling. Wayne also spent between twenty-five and thirty hours each week counseling families, something he was able to do because of the excellent staff his church board afforded him. During his years as pastor, the church visited every home within a three and one half mile radius to present the claims of Christ and invite people to put their trust in Him. The ministry in East Springfield also afforded him the opportunity to speak to pastor's seminars, denominational leaders and educators about applying the life principles put forth in the Bible to everyday life situations.

After twenty-six years of ministry in Pennsylvania, the Lord led the Augustine's to Jamestown, NY to pastor the Hillcrest Baptist church. There he and another pastor, Dayle Keefer of the Fluvanna Community Church (Dayle was also trained in part by Wayne's Dad) had the incredible opportunity to associate with and encourage over forty pastors in the Jamestown area in their ministries for Christ. These pastors worked together to distribute approximately 8,000 Jesus videos to the families of Jamestown, each pastor not focused on building his own church, but building the church of Jesus

Christ (the byproduct of which, more often than not, results in growth at home).

Upon resigning from the ministry in Jamestown, a pastor friend in Florida informed Wayne that the the Florida Conference of the Free Methodist Church was preparing to close a church in West Palm Beach and encouraged him to check it out. Upon meeting with the church board, the Augustine's began a nine year ministry in South Florida. Although much smaller than the churches he served in East Springfield and Jamestown, the Augustine's found this new challenge just as fulfilling as the previous ministries. They discovered that not where you serve, but being where God has called you to serve is what brings real fulfillment. The people of the church were a real blessing.

The Augustine's now reside in Wesleyan Village near Brooksville, Fl where they are committed to the success of the pastors there and serve in music and teaching ministries when called upon to do so. They have two sons, Timothy Wayne and James Percy, both of whom, along with their families, are committed to Christ.

Pastor James P. Augustine

James P. Augustine, the younger son of Wayne and Mary, was born on October 13, 1970. He lived in East Springfield, Pennsylvania the first eighteen years of his life. After six years of public school, he requested and was granted the opportunity to attend Girard Alliance Christian Academy where he graduated valedictorian of his class in 1989. He attended Moody Bible Institute in Chicago, IL and graduated in 93.

He served as a youth pastor at South Side Bible Church in Battle Creek, Mi. for ten years after which he and Cindy sensed a call to work with Campus Crusade for Christ. During the years of working to raise support for the ministry with Crusade, it became very clear that God had a reason for allowing them to struggle in their effort to raise support. They came incredibly close to completing their fund raising on several occasions, but then would lose ground. Several times they came to within $500 of completion, only to find several committed donors forced to stop their support due to economic reasons. God was leading Jim and Cindy toward His call to ministry.

The church they were attending was served by a wonderful pastor who was approaching retirement after twenty-nine years of faithful ministry and as the church prayed about his successor, several asked Jim if he might be interested. With great hesitation and apprehension, he and Cindy began to pray, realizing how difficult it would be to follow one who had had such an effective ministry for so long.

Jim presently serves as the Pastor of Faith Baptist Church in Battle Creek, Michigan. Faith Baptist is part of the Southern Baptist Convention.

Jim and Cindy, his wife, reside in Climax Michigan and have four children, Anna, age 12, Andrew, age 10, Abby, age 7 and Alexander, age 2.

11276975R00101

Made in the USA
Charleston, SC
12 February 2012